D1606390

THE BAGEL EFFECT

A Compass to Navigate Our Wired World

By
Paul Hoffert

**McGraw-Hill
Ryerson**

Toronto Montreal New York Burr Ridge Bangkok Bogotá
Caracas Lisbon London Madrid Mexico City Milan New Delhi
Seoul Singapore Sydney Taipei

McGraw-Hill
Ryerson Limited
A Subsidiary of The McGraw-Hill Companies

ISBN: 0-07-552923-8

1234567890 TRI 7654321098
Printed and bound in Canada.

Canadian Cataloguing in Publication Data

Hoffert, Paul
      The bagel effect

Includes index.
ISBN 0-07-552923-8

1. Organizational change. 2. Technological innovations 3. Social change.
I. Title.

HD58.8.H63 1998   658.4'06   C98-932421-4

Publisher: Joan Homewood
Editorial Co-ordinator: Catherine Leek
Production Co-ordinator: Susanne Penny
Editors: Jennifer Glossop and Lynn Schellenberg
Interior Design and Page Composition: Dianna Little
Illustrations: Eli Kassner
Cover Design: axyz fx
Cover Photo: Mike Smith and Chris Gordoneer

CONTENTS

ACKNOWLEDGEMENTS

Two of my colleagues at CulTech Research Centre, Dr. Jerome Durlak and Dr. Peter Roosen-Runge, were my sounding boards for Bagel Effect material and contributed their own ideas, many of which were incorporated into the text. My chairman and friend, Dr. Joseph Green, coached me for my early presentations and gave me free rein to spend endless hours researching, writing and speaking about the Bagel Effect.

The first draft was edited by Jennifer Glossop and the second by Lynn Schellenberg. David Hoffert helped shape the final draft with his insightful comments. Joe Mosher of NBTel reviewed the chapter on telephony. Mike Smith, creative director at BBDO, and photographer Chris Gordoneer shot the photograph that was used to anchor the cover design by John Fraser and Michael Schwabe of axyz fx.

The illustrations were done by Eli Kassner, whose unbounded talents take him to the top of professions ranging from classical guitar and visual arts to photo-micrography and moviemaking.

Don Berkowitz managed my book activities as if they were part of his job.

Brenda, my inspiration, and my children filled in, as usual, when my work pulled me from family responsibilities.

This book is dedicated to David Doze

PREFACE

In 1991, I founded CulTech Research Centre at York University. Its mandate is to investigate and solve problems at the intersection of culture and technology (hence the name Cul —Tech). To do so, CulTech must first identify the problems of today and then project the problems we are likely to face tomorrow. The most critical issues involve changes in social, economic, and industrial systems caused by upheavals in technology.

The advent of digital technology has enabled a new global economy based on the transfer and manipulation of information, which has been characterized as the Information Superhighway, or I-way. To chart the speed bumps along this road, I gathered a group of interdisciplinary thinkers who take a holistic approach to problem solving.

CulTech has been very successful at prototyping future communities, attracting resources to build them, and monitoring their behavior. The results in our trial communities have given us insights into how culture and technology intersect, and will help determine the best infrastructures for the future.

I first used the term "Bagel Effect" in public when I addressed the Advertising Research Council of Canada in November 1994. They asked me to predict how advertising would play a part in the new digital age. My colleagues and I at CulTech had been examining the phenomenon of control shifting from suppliers to consumers, and had successfully used this concept to predict Infoway development.

I coined the term Bagel Effect to describe this shift of power away from central administrations to individuals at system edges. I chose the bagel metaphor because when you diagram a system whose control leaves the center, it looks like a bagel. When I addressed the advertisers, I decided to step out and apply the Bagel model to their industry. At first, some of the agency execs thought I was talking about a chain of bagel shops. They began to catch on as I explained how television advertising would move from the current broadcast model to a narrowcast model with messages finely tuned to individual users. The question period was filled with thoughtful and provocative dialog.

The next month I was keynote speaker for the Canadian Real Estate Association. I used the Bagel Effect to frame expected changes in municipal taxation, funding shifts from federal to provincial governments, and increased use of the home as a place of work.

Soon I began looking at systems as diverse as politics, retail sales, and family lifestyle from the Bagel perspective. In each system, the conformation to Bagel Effect predictions was uncanny.

Businesses started to call and ask that I address their executives on how the changing environment would affect their profitability. In June 1995, I was a keynote speaker at a retreat for the Northern Telecom and Bell Canada executives. I used the Bagel Effect to describe a probable scenario for the telecommunications industry over the next few years.

In September 1995, I addressed the Cultural Industries Conference in Montreal. I spoke about trends in arts management from the perspective of the Bagel Effect. I suggested that government funding was on the verge of being decimated. It would be necessary to raise a much higher percentage of arts funding locally and from the private sector. It all made sense. Within a year of my prediction, government support to the arts was cut drastically.

Word was getting out about this weird Bagel predictor and I was inundated with invitations to speak.

The next month I was the keynoter for the Association of Municipal Officers — mayors and other senior officials from across the country. In November 1995, I represented Canada at the Organization for Economic Cooperation and Development in Paris, the economic forum for the developed nations of the world.

Then, in February 1996, I made a presentation to the Copyright Office in Washington, D.C., on the subject of managing intellectual property on digital networks. I used the Bagel Effect to design a system that accounts for every action, interaction, and transaction involving digital content, preventing piracy and ensuring that creators are fairly paid.

In all cases, the impact of my Bagel Effect presentations was very powerful. By the middle of 1996, my colleagues and I had applied the Bagel Effect to big-ticket items like education, health care, and telecommunications. Understanding how these sectors will change is worth trillions of dollars. The first fruits of this new understanding have given rise to new ventures producing learning materials, health management systems, video telephones, and entertainment-on-demand.

Using insight from the Bagel Effect, my colleagues and I have made many important predictions that have turned out to be correct. Frequently our conclusions were at odds with those of industrial experts. CulTech predicted the immense popularity of the World Wide Web, the primacy of computers (as opposed to TVs with fancy cable boxes) as interactive appliances, and the failure of movies-on-demand as a commercial venture. CulTech also predicted trends in education, health care, and personal communications years before they took place.

I have always been fortunate to be in the right place at the right time. I formed my rock group, Lighthouse, in the early '70s, just before the Canadian music business exploded. I helped found the Academy of Canadian Cinema in the early '80s, when Canadian moviemaking was moving into high gear. And I immersed myself in the field of digital content in the early '90s, just before the Internet took off. All of these moves were based on a gut feeling, but none felt so right as the Bagel Effect.

The book is intended as a guide, not an instruction manual. The Bagel Effect suggests that, although you may feel the world is spinning out of control today, you, as an individual, will gain control of your own opportunities in the coming years.

PART 1
A MEGATREND

A Compass to
Navigate our Wired World

As the millennium clock shifts its first digit from one to two (disabling most computer programs in the process), the impact of new technologies is becoming more pronounced but less understood. Fiber-optic networks, digital content, interactivity, and computers are bringing changes to our world as significant as those brought by the introduction of electricity, automobiles, telephones, sound recordings, and movies a century ago.

The changes taking place today are making innovation and information more accessible and more useful to ordinary people. But, like paddlers on a river narrowing to rapids, we're caught up in turbulence that obscures the calm ahead. We can see the end of danger only by stepping back and viewing the larger landscape — the factors influencing the chaotic flow.

The Bagel Effect describes how changes in technology, jobs, government, and family life can all be accommodated within a single understandable framework. It's the result of powerful forces that shape human nature and societies. The effects are massive and may be seen in every area of work and play. Wherever we look, we see shifting power, prosperity, and communities.

The Bagel Effect is the key to understanding these shifts. Think of it as a compass to navigate our changing and increasingly wired world. You can use the Bagel Effect to steer clear of obstacles in the uncharted seas ahead, and to direct you to your destinations. But, before you can fully make use of the Bagel Effect, you should understand the underlying struggle on which it's based.

1 THE BAGEL EFFECT
A Battle Between Freedom & Security

There's been a war raging ever since people became people, a conflict so basic to human nature that we frequently overlook it. We internalize this conflict every day from the time we're little kids until we die. As a society we externalize it in our communities, organizations, and governments. Sometimes the battle manifests itself as a war among nations, and sometimes it's expressed as the rebellion of a child against a parent.

On one side is our desire for *freedom*. On the other, our need for *security*. Motivated by these two basic instincts we fashion social, political, and economic systems that mirror our essential drives. History oscillates between periods in which one, then the other dominates.

Think about it. Freedom, risk, anarchy, chaos, choice, individual rights, free enterprise, free trade, and democracy are pulling in one direction. Security, safety, regulation, order, control, central authority, bureaucracy, protected markets, and dictatorship are pulling in the other.

Security	Freedom
Safety	Risk
Regulation	Anarchy
Order	Chaos
Control	Choice
Central Authority	Individual Rights
Bureaucracy	Free Enterprise
Protected Markets	Free Trade
Dictatorship	Democracy

Figure 1.1 - Security Versus Freedom

The forces of dictatorship, central authority, protected markets, regulation, and bureaucracy are associated with systems that have strong concentrations of power and controls at their centers. These forces are independent of political ideology. They are evident in both extreme left-wing (communist) and extreme right-wing (fascist) systems and represent social, political, and economic manifestations of our need for order and security.

The opposing forces of democracy, individual rights, free trade, anarchy, local authority, and free enterprise are associated with systems that have decentralized power with controls vested in individuals. They represent social, political, and economic manifestations of our desire to control our own destiny.

The Balance Point

As individuals and as communities we constantly struggle to establish an acceptable balance between these extremes. The right balance point allows some risk within overall security; freedom of speech and assembly balanced by regulations against hate-mongering and treason; local governments whose authorities are balanced with those of central governments.

BAGEL BITS

The Grateful Dead were one of the most successful groups in the history of popular music. Jerry Garcia, guitarist and spokesman for the group, espoused a philosophy of individualism and freedom that struck a chord with grassroots Americans from both the political right and left. But the Dead did not conduct their business in a chaotic manner. They coupled their message against government control and regulation with one of the most organized companies in the history of pop music. By combining sophisticated computer database management, direct marketing of concert tickets, and merchandising at concerts with an expressed culture of anti-government laissez-faire, they were able to reap millions from their ventures.

Constant Motion

People and organizations that find a good balance tend to flourish. However, in practice, this balance is rarely achieved because we live in constantly changing circumstances. We are governed in our work and leisure by many different systems — social, political, economic, religious, and others — each of which is constantly in flux. What may be a perfect balance today may be out of balance next week because events will have altered some aspects of each system. Like a pendulum constantly on the move, each system oscillates between extremes, with the result that we are constantly in a state of dynamic change.

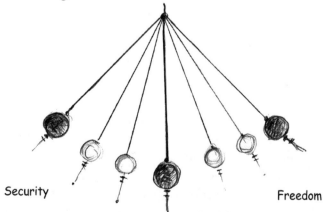

Security   Freedom

Figure 1.2 - Pendulum Swing from Security to Freedom

The only time the pendulum appears to stop is at the extremes, when its speed is least (zero) and its height is greatest. At one extreme, security is at a maximum and freedom is least, and at the other extreme, freedom is greatest and security is least. At each extreme, the system has the greatest potential to change direction. For example, when freedom is greatest, the forces of regulation and security are ready to restrict it, and when security and regulation are greatest, there is the greatest yearning for freedom. In a pendulum, this can be compared to the potential energy — the height of the pendulum — and the kinetic energy — the speed of the pendulum.

In the center of travel, each of the forces is in relative balance and there is a period of stability.

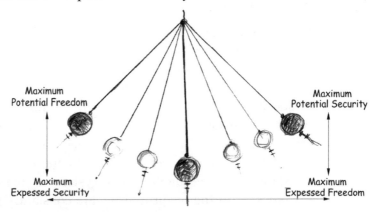

Figure 1.3 - Freedom Versus Security Cycle

Natural Cycles

As the pendulum swings along its course the opposing forces create cycles as one and then the other asserts itself. The same can be seen throughout nature where most systems are cyclic. Night and day, the lunar and menstrual cycles, and the seasons are all repetitive, cyclic, and essentially predictable phenomena. Because these systems are based on physically determined characteristics, such as the mass of the earth, the distance to the moon, or human life expectancy, scientists can analyze historic data and predict future behavior.

The stock market, fashions, and politics are just a few of the cyclic systems that help characterize our civilization. However, these cycles are more difficult to analyze and predict than natural cycles because they depend on characteristics such as human nature, the weather, and daily news, which are not very predictable.

Coincidence of Human Cycles

Many of the cyclic forces in our lives cancel each other out because their peaks and valleys of influence occur at different times.

From the moment of birth, certain internal biological cycles influence our actions and behavior. Our physical cycle is twenty-three days long, our emotional cycle is twenty-eight days long, and our intellectual cycle is thirty-three days long. These cycles are collectively known as biorhythms.

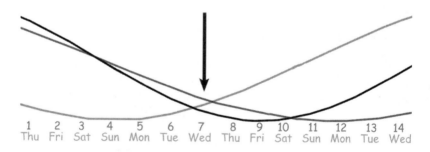

| 1 | 2 | 3 | 4 | 5 | 6 | 7 | 8 | 9 | 10 | 11 | 12 | 13 | 14 |
| Thu | Fri | Sat | Sun | Mon | Tue | Wed | Thu | Fri | Sat | Sun | Mon | Tue | Wed |

Figure 1.4 - Biorhythmic Cycles

When one of our internal biological cycles reaches its zenith or nadir we might expect to be at our best or worst, but the impact of a single cycle is often mitigated by the large number of other environmental factors around us. When several of our biological cycles reach their zenith (or nadir) on the same day, however, we perform measurably above (or below) par. The lesson here is that we are most likely to see change when several cycles are in supportive synchronization.

The Bagel Effect is the result, in fact, of important social, economic, and political trends peaking at the same time. As these systems come into alignment, they are reinforcing the movement away from regulation and security towards freedom and risk.

2 SUPPORTIVE SYNCHRONIZATION
Important Trends Combine

When several systems come into supportive synchronization — when their cycles are at a peak or valley at the same time — the linking influences become very strong and the effects are magnified. At the turn of the millennium, we are caught in a megatrend caused by the unusual synchronization of many important smaller trends whose motive forces are pushing and pulling together:

- Downsizing
- Decentralization
- Deregulation
- Digitization
- Convergence
- Interactivity

Megatrend Origins

The roots of the Bagel Effect began in the early 1980s as Ronald Reagan, Margaret Thatcher, Mikhail Gorbachev, and Deng Xiaoping began moving the United States, Britain, the Soviet Union, and China towards more open economies. Around the same time IBM introduced the personal computer, AT&T was broken up, and the United States opened its electric power grid to small, private suppliers.

In the early 1990s Western businesses and governments began to completely re-engineer their organizations so that decision-making was more distributed, middle management was reduced, and many tasks formerly performed within the organizations were now contracted out. This change in the balance of control within businesses has been mirrored in other areas of society by an increase in power for consumers, citizens, and clients at the expense of suppliers, governments, and bureaucrats.

Of greatest importance are two catalytic events that have fed the megatrend and broadened its impact. Taken together with the contributing trends of convergence, downsizing, digitization, deregulation, and interactivity they have had a massive and magnetic effect on other systems and brought them into synchronization. The catalysts were the fall of communism and the rise of the Internet.

Fall of Communism

The fall of communism created a huge shift away from central planning and control. It gave a big boost to free enterprise and democracy. This global change caused ripple effects in almost all systems and in our collective psyches. Communism was a formative force throughout the world. It proclaimed its future global dominance and predicted that other forms of social, economic, and political systems would fall on the scrap-heap of history. Its ideological attraction is undeniable, both in the underdeveloped world and in the developed democratic countries that echoed its ideology in the form of socialist and social democratic movements.

Key to the communist economic system was a series of five-year plans that controlled all aspects of the economy from a centrally planned model. There was no supply and demand. Only supply. Key to the political system was one party control and a totalitarian leader. Key to the social system was the idea that the collective community takes precedence over the individual.

When the communist system failed and the Soviet Union dissolved, the echoes were felt everywhere. The concept of regulated economies lost favor to the notion of free trade. And the ideal of the welfare state was replaced by increased individual responsibility for economic and social security.

In North America, politics has shifted towards smaller and less powerful federal governments and towards increased state and municipal control. Canada has eliminated its deficit by cutting spending dramatically, but the decrease in spending has come with a matching decrease in central power. The clearest indicator of decentralization in Canada has been the ongoing threat of Quebec seceding from the rest of Canada.

Rise of the Internet

In 1993, the Internet took off like a bat out of hell. Conventional wisdom held that people would not spend the time and energy to interact with their computers in order to get information and entertainment, but the World Wide Web proved that people liked to be interactive, given the opportunity.

The Internet is anarchic. It has no central administration. Its only means of regulation is by consensus. There is open access to all (provided you have the equipment) and it brings great risk for users because it lacks security. It has been compared to the Wild West before law and order were imposed. It is the antithesis of a controlled system and yet it has operated in a robust manner, grown enormously, and maintained excellent client relations.

The Internet captured our attention in part because our self-image has changed. We see ourselves as proactive individuals rather than passive consumers. The essence of the Internet is mirrored in our desire for more control over our lives. This fundamental shift in the way we view ourselves as individuals and as a society is having an enormous effect. We are taking more direct responsibility for our lives, for example:

- Parents are playing a larger role in their children's education;
- Individuals are saving for their retirement;
- Families are increasingly caring for elderly or sick relatives at home.

The Bagel Effect

And so these events and trends have set the stage for the megatrend of the century. The single system that incorporates important, distinct events and trends is easy to understand when you step back and look at the big picture. I call this system the *Bagel Effect*. The Bagel Effect describes power and control moving from system centers to their edges. It is itself a cyclic phenomenon currently at its maximum expression.

While words are good at conveying facts, images and metaphors are better for describing ideas. I use the image of a bagel as a metaphor for systems that express maximum freedom, and the image of a creampuff as a metaphor for systems that express maximum regulation. You might say that the Bagel Effect is the result of a movement away from creampuffs.

Creampuff Years

For most of my life, I've had to live in the shadow of creampuffs. While bagels are lean and nutritious, creampuffs are filled with fat and sugar in the center with only crumbs at the edges. The '60s and '70s were creampuff years when big systems reigned — big government, big business, big unions, big counterculture. It was a boom time for lawyers, accountants, and analysts — people trained to examine historic data and make logical judgments.

We're entering a period in which vision is paramount. When there is a changing paradigm, there is no reliable data to analyze. Like a jazz musician improvising a new melody on the harmonic framework of an old tune, we build our new future over the framework of the past, but the path requires creative improvisation. It's a time for extrapolation, not interpolation. And it's a time for creative thinking.

Forces, Systems, and Circles

Like all forces, freedom, security, and their relations act on systems to change them. Like the force of gravity that pulls a stone to earth when it's flung or centrifugal force that keeps water in a bucket when you swirl it at the end of rope, the cyclic elemental human forces act on all the systems around us. In order to better understand how these forces operate, it's useful to use the metaphor of a circle for a system. The circle can represent a system of technology, politics, economics, or human behavior. Things that are part of the system are inside the circle and things that are not part of the system are outside the circle. The circle acts as a confining perimeter between the system components inside and the non-system stuff outside.

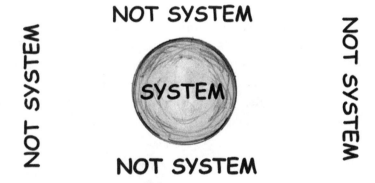

Figure 2.1 - System Inside, Not System Outside

Inputs feed the operation of a system. For a factory system, sales orders would be inputs. Outputs are the results of a system's operations, for example, manufactured products in the factory system.

The center of the circle is the system's core — its processes, administration, regulations, and controls. Those portions of a system that interact with inputs and outputs are closest to the circle's perimeter.

Figure 2.2 - Movement from the Center to the Edges

As administration, regulation, and control become decentralized, they move to the system's edges where they can interact with the world outside. This makes the system more open to interaction.

In many cases, the inputs and outputs of the systems involve people — clients, consumers, learners, citizens. In some cases the products may be intellectual property like entertainment or information. The center of the system might contain bureaucrats, administration, and processing technology.

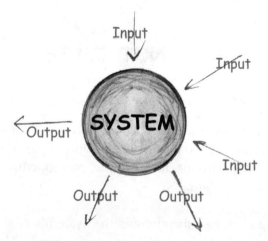

Figure 2.3 - Inputs and Outputs

Let's examine a record company as a system. The inputs to the system are master recordings. The outputs are music CDs. The processes include manufacturing the CDs, distributing them to warehouses, promoting and marketing them, and selling them to retailers, who ultimately resell them to consumers. These days a record company can put up a Web site that promotes the record, allows potential customers to sample the songs, polls them to determine which song should be targeted for radio airplay, and increasingly makes the sale directly through the Web site, delivering the physical CD by mail. This puts the marketers and promoters closer to the customers and decreases the company's reliance on intermediate distribution systems. Soon the music on the CD will be delivered directly to the customer over the network as a digital stream to be experienced live or recorded at home, eliminating the manufacturing process and record retailer entirely.

BAGEL BITS

Salespeople for the factory are near the perimeter of the system because they interact with inputs by taking orders for products. Shipping clerks are near the perimeter because they interact with outputs — they move products out of the system. The elimination of middle management positions in the shipping department may mean that the person who physically ships the product also communicates directly with the transportation company and even with the customer.

Shifting Power and Control

When a system loses all its central regulation, it becomes anarchic or chaotic. This can be described by removing the center from the circle — putting a hole in it. A circle with a hole looks a lot like a doughnut or a bagel. Of the two metaphors, a bagel better represents the lean and nutritious portion of the system that remains near the perimeter. The Bagel Effect describes this movement of power and control from the center of systems to their edges. It is evident in most of the systems that affect us.

The Bagel Effect

Figure 2.4 - The Bagel Effect

The Bagel Effect is manifest at the extreme end of the pendulum's travel where the forces for freedom, local control, risk, chaos, anarchy, democracy, individual rights, free trade, and open access are greatest. It is in this portion of the cycle that power and control are moving away from system centers. And it is in this portion of the cycle that we find ourselves at the turn of the twenty-first century.

Better Times Ahead

As the cycle reaches its extreme, the pendulum begins to retrace its path towards its center of travel and away from its instability. This is precisely where we are now in the cycle. The first decades of the twenty-first century will therefore bring more stability and prosperity than the last decades of the twentieth century. Others are also beginning to suggest that we are about to enter a golden age. In July 1997, Peter Schwartz and Peter Leyden wrote in *Wired* magazine: "We're facing 25 years of prosperity, freedom, and a better environment for the whole world." They cite the coming emergence of China as a major world market, the elimination of intermediaries in digital network transactions, and corporate downsizing as predictors of good economic times ahead.

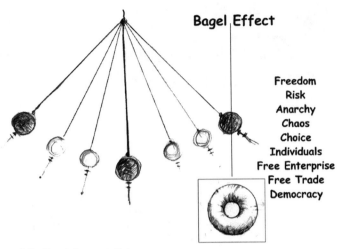

Bagel Effect

Freedom
Risk
Anarchy
Chaos
Choice
Individuals
Free Enterprise
Free Trade
Democracy

Figure 2.5- Pendulum at Extreme

These are, however, manifestations of the more significant Bagel Effect that will drive our economic, political, and social systems for the coming generation. The next chapter will begin to detail just how pervasive this megatrend is.

3 SHIFTING POWER
Consumers Take Control

It's a truism that history repeats itself. Although the critical events that enable change may be different in each era, human nature remains the same. The underlying issue we're examining — the battle between freedom and security — is no different today than it was thousands of years ago. We want the freedom to explore outside our immediate environment but we also need the security of our cave.

The cyclic nature of history can be seen as a pendulum swinging between opposing poles of centralized control and local autonomy. The French Revolution moved power from the monarch to citizens and the American Revolution moved it from England to the new local government. Seen in this light, the digital revolution is a repetition of past trends dressed in new technology garb.

Systems Are Connected

Natural systems are connected through their ecosystems and so in a sense are political, economic, and social systems. We speak of the free world and totalitarian governments being pitted against each other, as if they were discrete systems. In reality they are linked. In the case of the Soviet Union, the central controls imposed by the Communist system had strong impacts on Western economic and political systems.

The Soviet military build-up triggered an increase in military budgets and the power of the Pentagon in the West. It led to the Cold War and prompted the West to tighten its security and exert stronger central controls. In addition to the military echo, Western governments created welfare states that were just fainter echoes of Communism's central control.

Because history is cyclic, it's instructive to examine events and prognostications of a century ago when new technologies were also causing great upheavals in work and play. Then as now, few onlookers were able to discern the emerging patterns with any accuracy.

Electricity One Hundred Years Ago

When electricity was first introduced, there was a raging public debate between Thomas Edison who backed a direct current — DC — network technology and Nicholai Tesla who backed alternating current — AC — networks. (There is still a small part of Manhattan that's wired with DC because of Edison's misguided efforts.)

Although both AC and DC networks had their strengths, the overriding issues that supported the selection of the AC system in use today were input and output. Where would the power be generated and where would the users be? Because the power had to be generated hundreds of miles from users, AC won the day. Only alternating current technology could make use of transformers that step the voltage up and down as needed to overcome the natural losses encountered in transmitting power over long distances.

Once the AC/DC technology debate was over, everyone turned to the more important issue at hand: *Which electric applications would consumers find attractive enough to use and pay for?*

Those who supplied the light bulbs, radios, clocks, and refrigerators made huge fortunes while the central electricity network itself became a commodity business with government price controls. Like the Bagel Effect we're witnessing today, this system emphasized the elements at the system edges, in this case the appliances.

Current proponents of cable modems, fiber to the home, Internet via satellites, and so on vie for the attention of media and business. Which is the best network technology and which will predominate? The Bagel Effect suggests that consumers will become more empowered and be given more options with a greater variety of suppliers and network access technologies.

Within five years the major technical issues surrounding the new digital networks will be resolved and attention will once again focus on the key Bagel issue — system inputs and outputs: *Which digital applications will consumers find attractive enough to use and pay for?*

Those who will provide novel and useful things for users will earn fortunes while the networks that supply the raw digital capacity will fade into the background of public and media consciousness.

What's it all Mean?

The Bagel Effect is having a tremendous impact on major systems that affect every aspect of our lives. Following are some snapshots of this major influence at work. We will return to these examples in more detail in later chapters.

Bagels for Learning

One of the largest expenditures in government budgets is for education. Perhaps more than ever, there's a feeling that our educational systems are not preparing students for either the job market or for their role as contributing members of their community. In addition, colleges, universities, trade schools, training programs, and correspondence schools offer a collage of options that make it difficult for a student to assemble a cohesive lifelong learning program.

The Bagel Effect in education is taking control away from teachers and institutions and giving it to students. This shift in control will lead to more useful and lifelong learning, something that students want and need, and will demolish the educational system, as we know it. Education will be student-driven, featuring self-paced courses.

Bagels for Health

Health care is being put under a microscope in Canada and the U.S. from the dual perspectives of cost control and service delivery. The cost of prevention is much less than the cost of care and if we are to concentrate on prevention, control must move to individual users and away from the health care delivery system itself.

Experts agree that the majority of visits to doctors, health clinics, and hospital emergency centers can be dealt with outside the current institutional health system. It costs almost $1,000 less to care for a recovering patient at home than in a hospital, according to Saskatchewan's Health Services Utilization and Research Commission. Not only that, but in a two-year study, the commission determined that the shift in patient care from hospitals to homes for the last portion of convalescence also resulted in more satisfied patients.

Bagels for Earning

The Bagel Effect can be used to chart the best course for a business. In fact, it should help influence decisions about starting new businesses or winding down old ones. The downsizing that has gutted middle management in most companies has empowered employees at the edge — those closer to their customer inputs and outputs. For example, the employee who used to be one of ten workers reporting to a supervisor is now one of twenty. That employee has more responsibility and freedom to make decisions because there is less management (regulation).

Another interesting Bagel artifact is in the area of job creation. In the past, large businesses were the engine for job growth, but they have not created new jobs now for more than a decade. That task has fallen to the small business community. In fact, entrepreneurs at the system's edges are not only creating most of the new employment, they are starting new businesses and working out of their homes, a retreat from both big urban centers and big business practices.

Bagels for Consumers

The clearest example of the Bagel Effect in business today is the movement of power and control away from suppliers to customers. Companies that only a few years ago asked their customers, "Which of our products/services would you like to buy?" now ask customers, "What can we do for you?"

Consumers are taking power into their own hands by leaving brand loyalties behind and shopping for the best deals using all the distribution channels at their disposal. In March 1997, *Time Magazine* featured an article about consumers taking control from suppliers.

> Consumers — which are what America's hard-up wage-squeezed workers become in their off hours — have virtually seized control of many sectors of the economy. Food. Detergent. Clothes. Cars. Satellite dishes. All have become arenas of price wars in the past year for companies desperate to win customers. And the customers are making the most of it.

> Brand loyalty? No way. "Show us price and quality or beat it"... Jefferson Hill, managing director of the Meridian Consulting Group, says "Consumers ... are making a profound difference. In an economy that is far more deregulated and globalized."

Bagels for Governments

The Bagel Effect has been manifest in power shifting away from governments and political parties and out to citizens. National party loyalty has been eroding in North America for some time. In Canada, the 1997 federal election results were a puzzle to all but those who understood the Bagel trend. Regionalism clearly took over from centralism, as the federal government became an amalgam of five parties with only local support bases.

Governments are now admitting they cannot create permanent jobs. They have downsized greatly and, like businesses, are contracting out more work to the private sector. The devolution of power and control in the area of job creation, from big government to small entrepreneurs, is a clear indication of the Bagel Effect.

Bagels for Regulation

In many industries, the Bagel Effect is evident as a decrease in regulation or "deregulation," which allows more competition, lower consumer prices, and more choices for consumers. Currently we are in the midst of massive deregulation of the local and long-distance telephone services as well as the cable television industry.

Regulation itself is moving out of government centers and out to end users. In the field of telecommunications, the FCC in the United States and the CRTC in Canada are losing many of their regulatory powers as they slowly deregulate themselves out of existence. The regulation of television programs that contain sexually explicit or violent content is already moving from governments and TV networks to individual viewers who are gaining control over the types of programming that may enter their homes.

Bagels for Networks

The huge networks that crisscross our country with telephone, electrical, gas, and other utilities are being opened up to the connection of smaller local networks which can both feed into and take output from the large nets.

In the field of data communications, local area networks (LANs) now pervade large and small businesses and are rapidly taking hold in the home. These computer networks are already rivaling the telephone companies' wide area networks (WANs) in complexity and capability.

In the field of energy distribution there is feverish activity to build heating and cooling systems that can take multiple energy inputs — oil, gas, electric — so that consumers will be able to switch providers easily as the cost of a particular energy source becomes more or less competitive.

Bagels for TV

The market for broadcast television has been fragmenting significantly with the introduction of ever more cable TV channels. The major networks have seen a significant decrease in audience share. The trend is clearly towards many more specialty channels, each with a relatively small audience and a correspondingly small production budget. The bottom line is that the individual is gaining access to a wider variety of programming.

The evolution of broadcast television to interactive television is already taking place. As your set-top box evolves from a simple channel changer to an interactive Internet browser, broadcasters will lose control over program selection and scheduling, moving power and control to the edges of the television system.

Bagels for Telephones

Telephone companies — telcos — were taken by surprise by the huge consumer demand for wireless communications. They actually believed their business was about connecting telephones together through the network. Now they realize it's about connecting customers. Given the option of being tethered to a telephone in a fixed location or having the freedom to move about while communicating, the users have opted for freedom, a clear Bagel artifact.

The telephone networks were built with lots of control and intelligence at their central offices and little in the users' telephones. That architecture has been challenged by the Internet, which places intelligence and power at the edges of the network, in the users' computers. Telcos are grappling with the reality that selling bandwidth is becoming a low-margin commodity business in a competitive market. Telco shareholders are looking for more than that.

Bagels for Computers

One of the early manifestations of the Bagel Effect was the change in computer hardware from mainframes to personal computers. Many information technology officers and computer manufacturers missed the PC opportunity because they believed their businesses were driven by economics. While mainframes may be cheaper to own and operate, personal computers have taken over desktops because individual users have control over the interface, programs, and accessories. The shift away from central management of computing resources to distributed computing is a classic Bagel Effect shift. Users want to control their computers and they want to escape the tyranny of management information services — MIS —administrators.

The real Bagel Effect war is just around the corner, in the software arena. Microsoft has been controlling computer operating systems and applications for the past decade with its dominant Windows and Office software, but newer applications based on modular components are poised to take off in the coming years. This will give users the opportunity to pick and choose from the components to get the exact features they want and allow them to pay for only what they use — no more and no less. It will also allow them to select functional components from different vendors.

Bagel Effect — A Half-Century Swing

The current period for a pendulum swing is about fifty years. You can think of it as two generations of time: the first generation goes through the trauma of change and acclimatization, and the next grows up comfortable enough in the new paradigm to take advantage of it. Nobuyuki Idei, President of Sony, came to the same conclusion about time frame from a completely different perspective. In a *Popular Science* interview (April 1997) he says, "My theory is that each business cycle lasts 50 years, with one cycle overlapping another. The information age started 15 years ago and for the next 10 years it will be in the takeoff stage. Like a 747 nearing the end of the runway, it is still gaining speed ... after that you fly ... The job of the next generation is more important."

Taken individually, any one of the changes — the fall of communism, the changes in our health and educational systems, the shift in infrastructure from central to distributed computing, the deregulation of broadcasting and telecommunications, the movement of government closer to the people, or the emergence of the Internet as a global infrastructure — would be cause for re-evaluating our predictive frameworks. Taken together, and viewed within the context of synchronized cyclic change, they merge to create the biggest megatrend of the coming century.

PART 2
CONTRIBUTING
TRENDS

A Confluence of Disparate Forces

Several important trends contribute to the Bagel Effect megatrend. Each in its own right has large-scale impacts on our work, play, and governance. Together, their effects are even greater than the sum of their individual contributions. Like the biorhythms referred to earlier, the influence of these systems is more evident and predictable because they are in sync — peaking at the same time. They are linked in this chapter because they share many of the attributes of the Bagel Effect and may be seen as components of the Bagel Effect.

These trends are like mountain streams feeding the raging river called the Bagel Effect. Many of the characteristics of the streams are carried through to the river, but not all of the river's characteristics are found in each stream.

The contributing trends are:

- Downsizing
- Decentralization
- Deregulation
- Digitization
- Convergence
- Interactivity

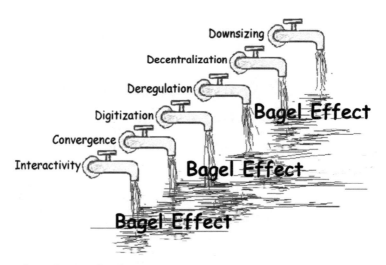

Contributing Trends

Although these trends originated separately, they resonate with each other because they share attributes, and particularly because the rise of the Internet, the fall of Communism, and the emergence of the Bagel Effect megatrend reinforce them.

The following chapters explain these contributing trends and set the stage for examining the social and industrial changes they are influencing.

4 DOWNSIZING
Less Is Right

Downsizing is the trend that has been sweeping through the public and private sectors in the last decade of the twentieth century. The creampuff years of the '50s, '60s, and '70s had produced companies, unions, and governments that were overstaffed and bulging with middle managers. They had lost contact with their customers, members, and constituents. In general, organizations had become less efficient and more inward-looking. They gauged their success by internal, industrial, and national rather than global standards.

But globalization was putting these organizations in competition with others throughout the world. In this international context, they came up short. Real estate, the stock market, and the general economy had been expanding for so long in North America that organizations had been able to maintain their operations within the illusory shelter of public confidence for a while before the roof caved in.

Finally, in the 1980s, reality struck. Japan, Taiwan, Korea, and other Pacific Rim countries caught up with the West's industrial technology and were able to produce and market goods more effectively. Western economies began to feel the competitive heat. As the automotive and other industries succumbed to the higher-quality and lower-priced products from the East, there were calls for protectionist measures to shore up local industries.

But the world was already en route to freer trade, and consumers rebelled against the raising of prices to compensate for industrial inefficiencies. Consequently, companies within every corner of the economy had to seriously re-evaluate their competitiveness. Because the economy had been booming for such a long time, it took a few cataclysmic events to embed the problem in the public's consciousness.

The savings and loan fiasco during the years of the Reagan administration softened up the public and the stock market meltdown in the late '80s provided the knockout punch. Financial losses were so high that companies had to shed vast numbers of employees to stay afloat. Almost across the board, large companies let go about 30% of their employees. The same middle-management positions that had increased in creampuff years were the first to go.

The name given to these massive layoffs was downsizing.

Downsizing Companies

Almost overnight, there was an acknowledgment that companies and workers had become complacent, that the work ethic had gone soft, and that drastic surgery was necessary to revive the North American economy. The downsizing solution was indeed drastic. Millions of employees were suddenly set adrift, sometimes a hundred thousand from a single company over a period of just a few years. It was clear that senior management wasn't going to be fired since they were managing the downsizing. Employees who were close to clients, those generating sales and building products, couldn't be let go without destroying a company's income. Everyone else in the middle of the corporate ladder was vulnerable.

The result of this massive corporate downsizing was that fewer people managed other people and a greater percentage of employees worked directly on producing and selling products and services. With fewer middle managers came fewer controls and more entrepreneurial spirit. Workers could make more individual decisions because they had fewer people looking over their shoulders, and because they had to make those decisions on their own. These power and control shifts were classic Bagel Effects, and they signaled the start of the megatrend's visibility.

Downsizing Governments

As people and companies made less money, they paid fewer taxes, and that exacerbated government budget deficits. Unaware that the Bagel Effect had already taken hold, governments kept spending as they did in the creampuff years, assuming that government could fix every problem with another new program. But increased government spending just made the deficit problem worse and eventually governments began realizing that, like companies, they needed to slim down significantly and shed employees.

National and provincial (state) governments had grown so large that they had become the most significant employers, a reflection of the years when the Soviet system had produced an echo of socialism in the form of large governments in the West. The downsizing of government has been particularly painful for public servants who lost their jobs. Many had entered public service expecting a lifetime of guaranteed employment.

Governments of every stripe are downsizing their bureaucracies and relinquishing some of their powers. This Bagel Effect influences everyone and every organization regardless of political ideology. In Canada, Prime Minister Chrétien's Liberal government has reduced federal spending and eliminated the budget deficit. In contrast, the Progressive Conservative government before it was the last of the big creampuff spenders. Even Ontario's former Premier Bob Rae, of the New Democratic Party, realized that it was paramount to decrease the size of the public service. He was doing the right thing at the right time, but it lost him his political constituency and the next election.

Downsizing and the Bagel Effect

The impact of government downsizing has been dramatic and contributory to the Bagel Effect. There are fewer government (centrally controlled) programs. Those programs that remain are administered by fewer individuals and generally have smaller budgets. Governments are less powerful today than they were a decade ago and they are continuing to limit their own power with new legislation like balanced budget amendments.

5 DECENTRALIZATION
Power to the Edges

"The choice is likely to be one of joining the revolution or being swept away by it. To survive, countless executives will have to overturn their own worldviews .... These people must decentralize their control."

— *The Cook Report* published on the Internet January 12, 1998 by COOK Network Consultants, Ewing, N.J., www.cookreport.com/building.html.

Decentralizing Companies

As companies downsized, they realized that many necessary tasks could no longer be handled internally because the expertise and human resources were no longer within the company. The result was that work needed to be contracted out.

By the 1990s, companies had redefined their work forces as a combination of full-time regular employees, and part-time contract workers. The full-time work force had gone from virtually 100% of the employees to about 85%. The Human Resource Institute did a study that indicated most firms expected no more than 75% of workers to have regular full-time positions by 2005.

The effect of the changing composition of the work force has been a decentralization of power and control within companies. Bosses who used to say *"I own you!"* had to watch their language (and thinking) lest they lose people with key skills on their teams who no longer were employees of the company.

This corporate decentralization was accentuated by the additional power that lower-level employees gained when their managers were fired. The movement of control to the edges of the corporate systems was a typical Bagel Effect.

Decentralizing Government

With a greatly reduced work force, it was natural that governments would cut programs. The cuts not only saved money, but also addressed the problem of no longer having enough public servants to administer the programs. The result was that governments became not just smaller, but weaker, as power and control leaked away along with the discontinued government programs and funding.

The domino effect was clear. Federal, centrally controlled governments ceded power to provinces and states, which in turn tried to offload costs and responsibilities to municipalities. Eventually many public programs, including social welfare, education, and health care, withered, leaving greatly expanded responsibilities with communities and individuals. This has been a very unpleasant transition for many people, but very predictable as seen from the perspective of the Bagel Effect.

The greatest impetus to weakening central governments was the collapse of the Communist Bloc of centrally controlled economies. Of the major nations, only China clings to the notion of a tightly controlled economy and even in this case, the country has enabled free enterprise zones whose success is washing over the rest of the country.

New Technology and Government Control

Later we will discuss whether technology is benign or evil. Within the context of weakening central governments, there is no doubt that the new connectivity technologies weaken governments' ability to wield power and control as they did in the past. In March 1998, FBI officials, frustrated by the limits that new communication technologies imposed on their wiretap capabilities, challenged the telecommunications industry to bring order and controls onto digital networks. They charge that "information that is critical to public safety and law enforcement will be lost". By that, they mean that wiretaps and other eavesdropping activities may be circumvented by the use of digital communications technologies like the Internet and digital wireless telephones.

Fax, wireless phones, computer, and Internet technologies played an important role in accelerating the demise of the Soviet system. The totalitarian system had relied on building physical and legislative walls around the state to keep out unwanted information about alternative and more prosperous free enterprise systems. The new technologies pierced the walls and let the unwanted information in. They also allowed for two-way communication with Westerners who built dialogues of friendship that broke down the natural fears of the unknown. Gregor Yavlinski, a leading member of the Russian Federation's State Duma, said, "Information certainly played a role in the collapse of the Soviet Union, as we got more and more information of how people were living abroad."

Problems for Governments

Throughout the world, the control of information goes hand-in-hand with power, and people are using their increased access to information to take power back from their governments. In January 1997 at the World Economic Forum in

Davos, Switzerland, Thabo Mbeki, South Africa's Deputy President, said, "Instant access to information brings new power to peoples along with new headaches for governments ... It's easier to govern if the population is ignorant."

Power to the People

In the United States, Congress has been dismantling federal programs and diminishing federal controls. There is a trend towards greater direct democracy by placing a growing number of legislative proposals on ballots. There have even been experiments using technology to instantly and economically register voters' preferences, allowing citizens to vote directly, instead of entrusting decisions to elected officials.

Decentralization and the Bagel Effect

Decentralization is a core attribute of the Bagel Effect — Movement of power and control away from the center of systems. The decentralization of companies and governments gives every indication of continuing over the next decade before it runs out of steam and begins cycling back towards centralized controls.

6 DEREGULATION
Greater Choice

"For regulators ... shock treatment is best. Get out ... technology will make it happen sooner than you dared hope."
— *The Economist*, April 4, 1998.

The movement from regulation to freedom is a defining aspect of the Bagel Effect. It is not surprising, then, that the global movement towards deregulation and free markets would play an important role in supporting and strengthening the Bagel Effect. Downsizing, which has decreased the pool of employees available to carry out regulation, has reinforced the trend towards deregulation.

As governments downsize and move towards free markets, there is a lessening of government regulation. People who buy goods, pay taxes, use computers, and watch television want to take more control of their personal environment. They want the government out of their lives and they resent the "big brother" attitude that was pervasive in the creampuff years.

Regulators Losing Power

Federal regulators like the CRTC (Canadian Radio-Television and Telecommunications Commission) in Canada and the FCC (Federal Communications Commission) in the U.S. are losing their central regulating powers. A bill was introduced by Congress to eliminate the FCC altogether. New technologies are also conspiring against government regulation. At the same time that citizens are asking governments to trim regulations, they are being enabled to self-regulate many of their activities using a computer designed to obviate central controls.

The trend towards deregulation began picking up steam in the 1980s when Ronald Reagan began deregulating sectors of the U.S. economy such as transportation. One by one, other regulated industries are being cut loose to compete as the rest of the economy does.

Free Enterprise Phase Two

Free enterprise is the bedrock of modern democratic economic systems. In the twentieth century, free economies were modified by ideas of socialism and social democracy, which resulted in greater government regulation. Sometimes the regulation actually encouraged freer markets, as with anti-monopoly laws. But in most cases the market sectors that have been allowed to operate in protected environments with government controls have been carved out of free markets and have reduced competition.

Power utilities, telecommunications, travel, and broadcasting are areas that were tightly regulated by governments within free market economies. We are now entering a second wave of free enterprise as a result of the deregulation of these protected industries through national and international legislation and agreements.

Free Trade

In place of international trade barriers that have regulated trade between nations, we now have free trade agreements that reduce government regulations and promote open access to markets. NAFTA (North American Free Trade Agreement) and GATT (General Agreement on Tariffs and Trade) are replacing tariffs and other regulatory impediments to free trade in Canada and the United States.

Deregulation has not been limited to North America. In 1997, countries throughout the world that trade in information technology agreed to deregulate their domestic telecom markets and abolish tariffs by signing the World Infotech agreement. This helped move the world's digital information flow into a free market that is spreading the technologies more quickly than ever.

More freedom! Less Regulation! Classic Bagel.

Trade Barriers Dropping Within Canada

Within Canada, the provinces have been working to abolish regulations that vary from province to province and hamper trade. States and provinces are reducing the complex regulations that impede interprovincial trade so truckers traveling cross-country can deal with harmonized laws about safety, loads, licensing, and so forth. Whereas the Bagel Effect encourages regionalism, it discourages regional restrictions to trade.

Small Companies Benefit

At a time when industrial giants continue to shed their workers, millions of small, dynamic companies are emerging all over the world. They are taking advantage of the deregulatory, decentralizing, and downsizing trends that provide fertile ground for sprouting newcomers who subcontract work from larger companies and frequently compete with them. These companies are creating jobs and spurring economic regeneration.

Deregulating Telephones

The deregulation of the telephone industry has already fostered new competition for your long-distance calls, which has led to a dramatic decrease in long-distance rates. Canadian telephone companies have had to shuck about a third of their staff. Local telephone service has been deregulated by the CRTC and we will soon see a wave of cable companies, satellite, and ground-based wireless companies trying to entice you to give them your local telephone business. The result of this deregulation process is more choice for consumers and less power in the hands of a few large businesses. Consumers rather than the telephone giants are beginning to drive the features and pricing of communications.

The implications are profound because corporate thinking in the telcos has always centered on the network and network services, but in the new paradigm, all the power is outside the network, with the consumer. The result will be a major realignment of suppliers of telecommunications connectivity and capacity with a corresponding redistribution of consumer spending.

Deregulating Broadcasting

The number of radio and television channels that can broadcast signals has been limited by the amount of electromagnetic spectrum available for this activity. The number of channels can be calculated by taking the total bandwidth allocated for broadcasting and dividing it by the bandwidth needed for a single channel. Governments have controlled the allocation of broadcast channels and imposed strict regulations on broadcasters to ensure that the public receives fair value for the scarce and valuable commodity that it is licensing.

But the advent of digital formats and digital compression has brought the availability of many more channels for voice, television, and data. In fact, with digital networks there is no use of the limited electromagnetic spectrum at all, nor is there any broadcasting in the usual sense of the word. Thus, the digital revolution brings with it a fundamental rationale for deregulating the broadcasting industries.

As the broadcast industry evolves towards a more interactive and user-controlled model, television and radio audiences will control the content that comes into their living rooms, playrooms, and bedrooms. The television industry has agreed to code programs for levels of sexually explicit language and images and for violence, so users may automatically exclude content they do not wish to see.

User Regulation

Objectionable programs will be limited by user choices and user filters, not by government fiat. The consumer can regulate contents by using digital hardware like the V-Chip available from cable companies or software like *Net-Nanny* to prevent undesired types of content from appearing on his or her TV or computer.

Information attached to programs will indicate the country of origin, languages available, suitability for children, levels of sexually explicit language and images, levels of violence, and so on. Adults will be able to regulate access to their own programs, and also to their children's.

Cable TV Revolt

Cable TV will not be spared the wrath of the consumer. Cable television has been a regulated monopoly. In each region a user is forced to take service from a single supplier if they wish to receive the multitude of channels not available through an antenna. This industry is also in the process of being deregulated.

The frustration and anger of customers being denied choice is bursting at the seams. In 1996, cable customers were enraged over the automatic delivery of new cable channels along with extra charges by some of Canada's cable companies. This so-called"negative optioning," which used the monopolistic power of the cablecos to set prices without consulting customers, triggered a consumer outcry and demands that the regulators speed up the entry of competitors to the cable companies.

Competition began in 1997 with the entry of satellite delivery of television programming and will continue as the telcos and others enter this business in 1998 and beyond.

Deregulating Energy

Japanese power and railway companies are already entering the Internet business. To an outsider this may seem strange because we don't associate these companies with digital networks. But the most difficult barrier that needs to be overcome if one wishes to construct a land-based digital network is the cost and complexity of assembling the rights to string the network cables over contiguous pieces of property from one end of the network to another.

Electric power companies have networks that reach into every nook and cranny of inhabited North America. Their towers may be used for stringing fiber-optical cables, and their existing power lines may be used to piggy-back digital electric signals. The major impediment to electric companies delivering telephone and data services has been regulation of these industries.

As deregulation takes hold in the energy industry as it has in the telco and cableco industries, new competition will arise for delivering all of these services. The consumer is certain to be the winner as choice and competition increase.

User Access to Electricity Grid

In 1997 Ontario Hydro made its first deal to buy energy from a private homeowner who installed solar cells on the roof of his home. On sunny days the homeowner sells power to Ontario Hydro. On overcast days and at night, he is charged for the energy he draws. His electricity meter is symmetrical.

It moves both forward and backward depending on the contribution to or pull from the utility grid. This concept of symmetrical systems in which users can also be providers is one of the new models causing headaches in boardrooms across North America.

Today you must decide on your energy source before you buy a water heater, stove, refrigerator, washer, or dryer. Choosing electricity, gas, or oil as your energy source dictates which appliances you can buy, and which supplier can provide your energy. These days are numbered as the energy industry enters further deregulation.

Deregulated energy will result in a proliferation of plans, deals, and options designed to appeal to individual users, not the one-rate-fits-all system that we're used to. Coming soon are appliances that will take multiple fuel types as their energy source: for example, a water heater you can connect to electric, gas, or oil sources. You'll check out the prices of energy on a regular basis and be able to change energy types and suppliers according to the best deal available at the time — just as you do with your long-distance phone service.

Recently, the chair of a major energy utility summed it up,"There will no longer be captive consumers like we used to have. They are no longer ratepayers. They are customers."

Keeping the Internet Unregulated

Those that would impose controls on this anarchic system are attacking the Internet, the world's first perfect Bagel. But in July 1997 the Supreme Court of the United States struck down this attempt as unconstitutional and a limit on free speech. The Bagel Effect predicts that the Internet will remain without significant regulation. But as the Internet splinters into business-oriented intranets (see Chapter 11, "The Rise of the Internet"), these will bring all sorts of regulation with them, including the much called for regulation of hate and sex Web sites.

Deregulation and Consumerism

A new age of consumerism is being heralded by deregulation and it is already exhibiting characteristics of the Bagel Effect as users gain more freedom to choose and more overall control. The next twenty years will see a much greater impact from deregulation as these enormous industries re-engineer their businesses to deal with the new reality of increased competition.

7 DIGITIZATION
The New Revolution

What Is Digital, Anyway?

We learn to count using digits — fingers and toes. Digital systems are similar to our body parts in that they correspond to exact numbers of things. Defining a room as twelve feet by twenty feet with an eight-foot-high ceiling is more exact than saying, "It's a good-sized room for family activities."

However, we perceive the world in analog terms, not by quantity but by quality. We say it's a bright day, not that the luminosity is a certain number. Until recently, most recording and storage systems were analog; that is, they approximated natural systems without reducing them to numeric quantities. The squiggles on a phonograph record and the waveforms of a television broadcast are examples of capturing sounds and images in analog formats.

Digital technology, on the other hand, reduces phenomena to simple numbers. Sound volume or image brightness may be expressed as an exact number that relates to the highest achievable level.

BAGEL BITS

The highest sound level on a compact audio disc is defined as 65,536 units. The number 32,768 then represents a sound level half as loud as the maximum level. Any characteristics of a system may be expressed in digital terms.

Text is digitized by assigning a number to each letter of the alphabet. If we count upper case letters as different than lower case and add the assortment of punctuation, accent, and other markings, we can still represent all text characters with no more than 256 numbers. In digital parlance, this is eight bits or a single byte.

In order to describe quantities that vary with time such as music and moving pictures, successive loudness or brightness levels are captured at regular time intervals called frames. Television frames are captured every 1/30th of a second, compact audio disc frames are captured every 1/44,100 second.

A key differentiator between digital and analog technologies is that digital allows the expression of different phenomena with the *same* system of numbers and that makes it possible to process and distribute any digital signal with the same equipment, an enormous benefit. It explains why you can use your computer's disk (floppy or CD-ROM) to store a game, a book, or music.

The Binary System

The most common base for a number system is ten — the decimal system. Ten ones are ten. Ten tens are one hundred, ten hundreds are one thousand, and so on. The reason for choosing the number ten is that we have ten fingers and toes. But ten is not a particularly useful number base for counting things other than fingers or toes. Many natural phenomena have natural bases other than ten.

There are twenty-four hours in a day, three hundred and sixty degrees in a circle, and so on. Digital systems generally use the binary system of numbers because computer memories consist of tiny electronic elements that can be flipped on or off like a light switch. You can think of the light switch as having two states, on and off. These can be represented by the two digits 0 and 1.

The binary system has become the fundamental format for storing and transmitting digital data because of its simplicity and because the binary digits may be stored, processed, and distributed by any digital appliance, network, or processor. Thus, you can store audio, video, and text on a computer disk, whereas you'd need a videotape, a phonograph record, and a book to do the same in analog formats. In fact, there's no easy way to integrate the analog information from a book, videotape, and phonograph record into a single medium, even though they may be on the same topic.

One of the first popular digital appliances was the digital watch. It uses the same underlying technology of 1s and 0s used in computers. Because of this, you can buy a watch that communicates with your computer, and downloads telephone numbers, addresses, and messages to your wrist.

Digital Technology and Bagels

The fact that all digital data is reduced to a simple, standard, and interoperable format encourages the exchange of information. Digital systems are intrinsically more open to access from a wider range of suppliers and users.

The other side of accessibility for an open and standard data format is the relative ease with which hackers and pirates can break into such systems. As a result, digital technology has spawned industries that focus on protecting valuable digital data and systems.

Digital Distribution Is Global

Digital technology is special among the great twentieth-century technologies because it seems capable of revolutionizing every aspect of work, family, and leisure time on a global scale.

The new digital distribution systems are pan-national. Since there are no customs booths to intercept digital signals as they travel from country to country, the new transmission channels open world markets to anyone with access to them. Access to digital distribution is intrinsically cheaper and more available. Physical distribution systems require warehousing and transportation that present enormous financial barriers to all but a few large companies, but digital infrastructure has become available to anyone wishing to use the distribution infrastructure at very affordable rates.

Since services can be delivered across territorial boundaries while circumventing regional and national protective barriers, digital technology encourages free trade. The digital revolution is yet another trend that increases freedom and decreases regulation, consistent with and contributing to the Bagel Effect.

Digital and Industrial Revolutions

Let's compare the industrial and digital technology revolutions. The industrial revolution altered every aspect of people's lives. It changed the workplace and invented the description of a job, as we know it. It changed family life, the way we do business, the way government is run, and it created the infrastructure necessary for modern civilization. Roads and canals had to be built to transport factory-produced goods that were now too numerous to be absorbed into the local economy.

Digital technology promises to do the same. It has already changed the workplace and jobs by allowing workers to do many of their jobs at home while connected to their office. It has also enabled a new and growing class of small businesses operating from home offices.

Digital technology is changing family life as children do their homework at home computers and their parents use the Internet for everything from shopping to planning their vacations. Television, one of the greatest cultural influences on families, is moving to digital technology, which will allow it to interface with computers and digital networks.

Digital technology has greatly increased the information flow from governments to businesses and ordinary citizens. More importantly, governments are getting much more feedback directly from citizens via e-mail and other digital technologies. Every politician maintains a Web site and uses it to interact with their constituents.

Most important, a new digital infrastructure is crisscrossing the globe. It may have even greater impact than our physical system of roads, highways, shipping lanes, and air routes, because anyone anywhere on earth will have equal access to the digital transport system as satellite, cable television, telephone, and wireless technologies branch out into every nook and cranny of civilization.

Naysayers

During the industrial revolution a small but vocal group violently opposed technology change because it put many workers out of jobs and exploited others. These Luddite radicals swore they would prevent the implementation of the new mechanized technologies. They were honorably motivated but doomed to failure because the creation of new tools is an essential hallmark of human activity. Using technology distinguishes humans from other animals. It is therefore inappropriate to characterize the introduction of technology as dehumanizing, and to expect that people will not use it.

Nonetheless, certain groups are opposing the introduction of digital technology as if it were a Trojan Horse, part of an elaborate plot to co-opt human integrity and substitute inhumane and uncaring values in its place. These groups, like the Luddites, will fail to stop the implementation of the new technologies. They should take a lesson from history. There are no records of technologies that were not implemented, provided they improved the quality, efficiency, or novelty of work and play. Digital technology meets all of these tests.

BAGEL BITS

The introduction of fire technology in prehistoric times caused great changes in the balance of power among those who had access to it and those who did not. Those who didn't have fire were marginalized and may not even have survived. Fire brought great improvements to the quality of human life and no one has managed to extinguish its utility. The same may be said for other technological innovations. Human societies are ever in flux, dynamically exchanging power and control from one group to another, frequently as a result of advances in technology.

People Cause Change. Technology Only Enables It!

Technology, digital or otherwise, enables changes but does not produce them. Only people produce changes and that's why the key to understanding the coming decades is not technology, it's human nature.

You don't have to learn about digital packets to understand where we're headed. The action is at the edges of the digital networks — the input of content and the output to users. When the Bagel Effect is operative, suppliers and distribution are less important than users.

Those who are concentrating on the bits, bandwidth, and atoms are missing the essence of the new, changing paradigm. The emphasis has moved from the center to the edges of the networks, to the people acting, reacting, and interacting with the content.

Digital Technology Is Neither Good nor Evil

Some people fear that digital technology is inherently "evil" and dangerous. Others believe that the digital revolution is inherently "good" because it fosters greater and more democratic access to knowledge. But the evidence is that technologies themselves tend to be neutral. It is human behavior as it uses technology that is good or bad. Fire may be used to heat a home, cook food, or burn down a rival's home. A knife can be used to cut food or to commit murder. The tools aren't good or bad. But they can be dangerous in the hands of those who are unaware of their dreadful potential (children) or those who would use them for evil purposes.

Similarly, neither mechanical nor digital technology is essentially good or evil. Both have the power to do enormous good or evil in hands of good or evil people. Like printing, digital technology can be used to disseminate information and impart knowledge or it can be used to disseminate hate literature and child pornography.

Patterns of Implementing Technology

My Concerto for Contemporary Violin was recorded in 1979 using a then-new technology called direct-to-disc. This new technology caught the interest of Marshall McLuhan who wrote the liner notes for my record, including the following comments about implementing new technologies. I believe it was the first time he published this now-famous analysis. He said:

> ...Contrary to popular thought technology is very humanistic. Every new technology goes through four phases as it is introduced:
> It enhances something
> It obsolesces something
> It echoes an earlier technology
> It flips into a new and contradictory form

Digital technology has been following exactly this pattern.
- It enhances data processing and storage, connectivity, and so on;

- It obsolesces analog technology;
- It echoes phonographs, telephones, televisions, and so on;
- It is flipping into new contradictory forms like the Internet.

BAGEL BITS

If we learn a technology when we're young it becomes invisible and comfortable to us, like cutting food with a knife or writing with a pen. A new technology is usually presented to us after our formative years when we've matured but before the technology has. Because the tool is new it presents us with awkward and immature interfaces. We are required to learn to use the tool at a time in life when our brain patterns are already formed and so we find it difficult to learn new skills. Digital technology may strike some people as difficult and frustrating but the problem is generational. Kids take to computers, the Internet, and interactive games like ducks to water. These and other activities brought about by the digital revolution are as transparent to them as using a telephone is to their parents.

Being Digital — Negroponte Is Wrong

In 1995 Nicholas Negroponte, director of MIT's Media Lab, wrote a book called *Being Digital.* Coming from an institute of technology, he was caught up with the importance of engineering and technical systems. The book's central theme is that to understand the important changes taking place you must focus on the difference between atoms and bits.

But the new paradigm doesn't give much weight to technology. It focuses rather on input and output — the content fed into a system and the way people use it at the system edges. From this perspective you don't have to understand the difference between atoms and bits any more than you need to understand the difference between amperes and kerosene to turn on a light.

In my view, *Being Digital* is a wrong-headed approach to understanding the impact of digital technology. The last thing we need is to be digital. People will never be digital. People should never be digital.

Let's compare digital technology to the electricity network, the most important technology introduced in the last century. You don't need to understand electromagnetic theory to use a toaster or a light bulb. You gauge the value of electricity by the appliances it enables, not by understanding the electrical network.

This book may serve as an antidote to Negroponte's book. You can be very successful in these changing times by retaining your analog nature while seizing the opportunities afforded by new digital technologies.

Where Will Digital Lead?

It's hard to predict the impact of the digital revolution. When automobiles were introduced as replacements for horses and carriages, no one imagined that they would lead to changes in the structures of cities. Just as it was difficult to predict that automobiles would create new communities neighboring on cities — suburbs — it is difficult to predict the effects that new digital technologies will have on communities.

The Bagel Effect points to some probable scenarios including the invigoration of smaller and rural communities for whom digital connection can mean a shift from being marginalized at the edge of our civilization to being at the power center. As with other technology revolutions, those who sit on the sidelines become marginalized, while others who embrace the technology become more powerful.

Digital Technology Leads To Convergence

We've seen how downsizing and decentralization have invigorated the trend of deregulation. Next we will examine how the trend of digitization has led directly to convergence, one of the major trends at the end of the twentieth century and a key contributor to the Bagel Effect.

8 CONVERGENCE
Digits Bring It All Together

"The consumer electronics industry would like to see every device it makes have a unique Internet address as soon as possible."

— Dr. Hiroshi Fujiwara, President and CEO of the Internet Research Institute, Japan.

Because televisions, automobiles, and stoves all use digital processors, it's possible to link them using digital computer networks, provided they can be identified and communicated with. Dr. Fujiwara and others suggest that the Internet be the linking network and that Internet addresses be used to identify the individual appliances. This would enable previously separated systems to interoperate, an example of *convergence*.

Convergence is being driven by digitization. Together they may be thought of as the core of the digital revolution. Convergence is taking place in formats, media, appliances, distribution channels, markets, and industries. The many forms of convergence are a consequence of content digitization — information, books, music recordings, movies, watches, telephone switches, heating controls, light switches, telephones, security systems, television sets, cellular phones, computer networks, and so on.

The most common use of the term convergence refers to the interoperation of the television and telecommunications industries. Convergence in this case has been driven by the digitization of:

- Telephone conversations, data, and telecommunications equipment;
- Television signals;
- Audio and video production facilities.

The result is that telephone companies can now deliver television programs through their networks and cable television companies can now deliver telephone service through their networks.

The convergence of these two industries is just the tip of the convergence iceberg that is drifting towards every industrial ship that drives our economy.

Convergence and the Bagel Effect

It is reasonable to ask why convergence contributes to the Bagel Effect when it might be seen as restricting the choice of formats, media, distribution channels, and appliances. In fact, convergence is a contributing trend to the Bagel Effect because it makes it easier for users to get the services and content they want. By rationalizing formats, media, and distribution channels to fewer but more standard formats, convergence allows many more suppliers to make their products and services available and at a lower price to the consumer. By placing suppliers and consumers closer to each other, convergence diminishes the power and control that has been vested in proprietary and closed formats, media, and distribution systems.

Deregulation has contributed to the impact of convergence by eliminating distribution monopolies and increasing the number of digital distribution channels available.

BAGEL BITS

The single distribution channel for cable television and the single distribution channel for telephony are burgeoning into many consumer options for receiving digitally converged services and products, including wireless telephony, satellite delivery, telephone lines, cable TV lines, and power lines. The results have already demonstrated lower prices to users and a greater variety of content and services. This translates into greater freedom and power to consumers, a clear Bagel Effect.

From Divergence to Convergence

Convergence has arisen as an important trend just in the nick of time. It has become impossible to keep up with the wealth of information available in the twentieth century. It wasn't always so. The Renaissance held as its ideal the person who could write a sonnet, play a musical instrument, be fluent in the sciences, and manage the family business. An intelligent citizen could know pretty well all there was to know and might engage in meaningful discourse on the issues of the day, be they politics, science, religion, family matters, or the technology of war.

But the end of the Renaissance marked the end of a holistic view of culture and technology. As generations passed, the amount of information increased and there began an accelerating trend of information production and specialization. The introduction of the printing press and the corresponding notion of democratic access allowed many more people access to information and a means to share it.

Specialization and Information Overload

In the nineteenth and twentieth centuries public libraries and public schools further opened the information system to input and output from a growing number of literate individuals, setting the stage for the information overload we experience today.

Now, at the crossroads of millennia we are immersed in an ever-increasing spectrum of interests and specialization, caused by having more information than we can assimilate and process. It is no longer possible to know everything. It is no longer possible to know everything even in your field of interest. In fact, specialization has gone so far that experts know almost nothing outside their field and in the case of our brightest minds, they are frequently focusing on problems of such specificity that almost no one has the contextual background to fathom what they are talking about. As an example, the average number of mathematicians who read an article in a peer-review journal is less than two persons. That includes the author.

Holistic Thinking

If we are to tunnel through the mountain of data into a more manageable future, we must compress the ever-expanding number of subjects into fewer, broader, and more manageable categories. Fortunately, with the various forms of convergence taking place, we are returning to more manageable and holistic approaches. The reversal of specialization and the re-emergence of big-picture thinking are beginning to produce important solutions to difficult problems.

Format Convergence

As we've seen, an important aspect of digitization is that on the lowest level, the digital data format is identical for all information — 1s and 0s. This may be viewed as a convergence of formats to a single basic binary digital format. Digital data may be structured in a variety of protocols and standards according to the context that is required by the users' appliances.

On a higher level, digital formats are converging as well. Incompatible network protocols that were used for the television, telephone, and data communications industries have now converged to a few protocols that accommodate all of voice, data, and video.

BAGEL BITS

A compact music disc structures the 1s and 0s to indicate the song titles, the names of the artists and composers, and the song durations, while an e-mail message structures the 1s and 0s to indicate the sender's and receiver's addresses, length of the message, and so on. In both cases, the content may be stored on fixed media like a compact disc, removable media like a floppy disk, in a computer's memory, or distributed across a digital network.

Content Convergence

Content convergence refers to information and entertainment that can be delivered on digital media and networks. The first content to converge to digital formats originated on computers as text and numbers, the least complex content to represent digitally. The industries involved are banking, stock and bond trading, research services, periodicals, government information services, and news libraries. They have benefited from the Bagel Effect, moving customers closer to products and services, and eliminating bureaucracy in between. These industries will continue to prosper because they provide information and services targeted to individual customers.

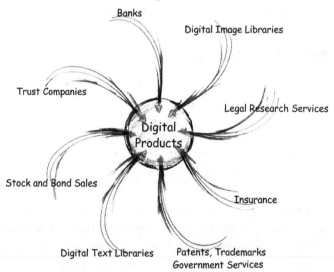

Figure 8.1- First Wave Content Convergence

Books, magazines, and newspapers are in this content category but are converging more slowly because their paper-and-ink media are better suited for delivering content on a bus, at the kitchen table, or in a waiting room.

The second category of digital content consists of products that are more complex to convert than text and numbers. Audio and video in the form of music, movies, and multimedia are being converged to digital content formats that allow them to be stored, transmitted, and presented by the same systems.

Digital content that has been expressed in audiocassettes, music CDs, computer programs, computer games, photographs, artworks, talking books, videodiscs, and videotapes is being converted to digital formats such as Acrobat, JPEG, MPEG, HGML, and html. After conversion, the content can easily be processed, searched, sorted, enhanced, converted, compressed, encoded, replicated, and transmitted by digital information systems.

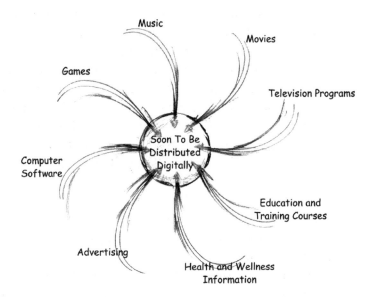

Figure 8.2- Second Wave Content Convergence

Media Convergence

In traditional media, you can't deliver music within a newspaper any more than you can deliver a book within a videotape. In the new digital media, however, you can deliver these and other content categories, such as movies and simulations, within the same converged media. An example of such media is the compact disc.

Example — Compact Disc

Music recordings were the first consumer products to go digital. The introduction of the compact disc in 1983 affected many industries. Electronics companies began making CD players, pressing plants were built to produce the new plastic CDs, record companies converted their master recordings from analog to digital, music production studios replaced their audio equipment, and retailers had to build new display shelving because CDs are smaller than LPs. That makes CDs easier to steal, so store security systems also had to be redesigned.

As the music industry switched to CDs, the unit cost of manufacturing them went down dramatically — from about a dollar and half at first to about sixty cents today. CDs cost only a little more than computer floppy disks, but they have five hundred times their capacity. Consequently, computer software manufacturers began using CDs to deliver their programs, which were already in digital formats. CD manufacturing volume went through the roof, while manufacturing plants making floppy disks were marginalized.

Kodak, the largest manufacturer of photographic film and leader in photo-finishing, decided that the same CDs used for storing music and computer programs could be used for storing digitized photographic images. Kodak introduced the Photo CD format that allows images to be stored on compact discs, and they designed equipment to translate photographs on film into digital images. The result is that fewer prints are processed in the traditional way with chemicals, which in turn reduces demand for products from the mining and chemical industries. The increase in the production of CDs consumes more plastic, however, which boosts demand in the oil industry. Many new pressing plants were built to meet the increased demand for CDs.

Once photo-shops had the technology to store and process digital images, camera manufacturers were encouraged to develop and market cameras that record images directly on digital media instead of film. Now you can display photos on your computer screen or television set directly from your camera, as photographic media converge with computers and television.

The next generation of the CD is the DVD. A DVD is the same size as an original CD but with much greater capacity. It can store a complete movie in digital form, for example. The film industry calls the DVD a Digital Video Disc, and will use the format to replace videotapes and videodiscs. The computer industry dubbed it the Digital Versatile Disc and uses the same medium for storing computer data. DVD movie players debuted in 1997 and in 1998 for computers.

Recordable CD and DVD technologies were developed so users could write information to the discs as well as read information from them. Their popularity has been so great that the cost for a blank recordable CD dropped from ten dollars in 1997 to about a dollar in 1998.

So, in addition to the industries that produce music, consumer electronics, computer software, cameras, photographic supplies, and the CDs themselves, we now have the Hollywood movie industry, videotape duplicators, and video rental stores converging to the same digital medium. The upcoming increase in volume for the compact disc format will bring prices down for the consumer even further.

CDs are in tune with the Bagel Effect. When Phillips and SONY developed music CDs, they could have kept the format proprietary and closed to competition. That would have made the CD a creampuff medium, tightly controlled by suppliers. Instead, the inventors made the CD a public and open standard. Public standards are very Bagel-friendly because they move control toward consumers and provide for access that is more democratic. Phillips and SONY allowed other manufacturers to use and modify the technology. The result is that the CD format has the lion's share of the market and has expanded to the new DVD format.

On the other hand, when SONY introduced its Mini Disc and Phillips introduced its digital audiocassette formats, they were proprietary closed standards, and both failed in the marketplace. It's a sign of the Bagel Effect when retailers and consumers quickly squash industrial efforts at monopolistic control.

Appliance Convergence

Television sets are designed to operate comfortably in a family room whereas computers are designed for a work environment. Neither appliance is suitable for use in the kitchen, say, delivering recipes while you're preparing a meal. Neither is user-friendly in the bathroom, where you may want to read the morning's digital newspaper. Neither could be used to give you directions while you're driving your car.

Yet we continue to be caught up in the question of which appliance will win the battle for supremacy. In truth, TVs and PCs are converging to a single appliance that will be capable of displaying both television and computer images well, but the social utilization of that appliance has been given almost no thought, even though it remains a key determinant for the future of computers and televisions.

Products like Web TV allow you to access the digital Internet on your television set and products like QuickTime allow you to play videos on your computer. These are just the first wave of what will be a host of new appliances that will be suitable for the new varieties of digital content.

We have yet to see the appliances that will flip into (Marshall McLuhan's) newer and contradictory forms. Computers and television sets have been touted as the information appliances of the future, but it is unlikely that either of these appliances will survive, as we now know them.

Marketing Channel Convergence

Even industries that sell products that can't be digitized are benefiting from the convergence of marketing and sales networks. The sale is made using a converged network such as the Internet. Then conventional mail or courier, known in the digital trade as SneakerNet, delivers the physical goods. Today, high-value goods like computer equipment, books, and recordings are being sold using converged marketing channels. Soon, products like pizza, milk, toilet paper, tins of soup, and socks will increasingly be sold through these channels because consumers can easily browse the network for the best price and have the merchandise delivered to their front doors.

Many goods lend themselves to being displayed and auditioned over networks, then delivered by SneakerNet. The sale of music CDs from Web sites made a breakthrough in 1998 as consumers listened to portions of compact disc songs on the Internet, then ordered the CDs for delivery by mail. More than 10% of the $15 billion annual music CD sales have now moved from retail stores to the Internet, a new converged marketing channel.

Industrial Convergence

Industries whose products and services have been digitized are already converging. Their products are being distributed along the same routes, to the same appliances, and to the same customers as their new competitors' products.

Businesses such as computers, telecommunications, cable and satellite television, consumer electronics, music, video, catalog shopping, gaming, banking, financial services, book and magazine publishing, advertising, education, and health care will increasingly cross over into and poach each other's markets.

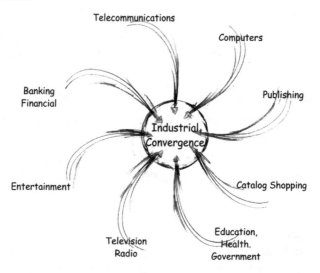

Figure 8.3 - Industrial Convergence

Example — Telcos and Cablecos

In 1998, the North American cable television industry earned revenue of about $20 billion while the telephone industry earned $200 billion. The telcos had the digital switching capacity to route any signal to any home but the bandwidth of telephone lines is too low to send television-quality signals. The cable TV system uses coaxial lines which can carry television but can't switch signals to individual customers.

If the phone system and cable system collaborated, they could use the telco switching capability with the cableco bandwidth to deliver switched broadband entertainment and communications to your home. But the competitive nature of telcos and cable companies — cablecos — has prevented them from collaborating, even though regulators like the

CRTC and the FCC have been opening the door for such alliances. In 1998, AT&T, the largest American long-distance telephone company, announced a merger with TCI, the largest American cableco. They plan to use the switching capacity of the telco with the bandwidth capacity of the cableco to offer high-speed Internet and other broadband services to their customers. This will result in a significant convergence of distribution channels.

Distribution Convergence

Each type of convergence — format, content, media, appliance, market, and industrial — supports the new digital distribution channels. Today these channels are comprised mainly of the Internet and private networks like America On-line. Tomorrow there will be many digital distribution channels through which retailers and wholesalers will make their products and services available to the world. Digital networks will be the preferred conduits for all information, entertainment, products, and communications.

Convergence, Regulation, and Bagels

It is important to note the relationship between deregulation and convergence. Without deregulation, convergence might have the effect of concentrating more power in the hands of a few large suppliers of connectivity and content. Instead, the deregulatory trend is weakening the large connectivity suppliers who have to increasingly compete for their market shares. It is questionable if the major telephone, cable, and utility companies will be able to survive intact, much less retain their dominant control over the pipelines to our homes and businesses.

Although distribution of all manner of content is converging to a single digital channel, the distribution market is fragmenting among many suppliers. Some own parts of the digital infrastructure and others just lease bandwidth from owners, putting together virtual networks like the small long-distance companies do today. This is very Bagel-friendly because it gives consumers more choice and drives down prices.

This Is Big Stuff

This is big stuff. North American video rentals account for more than $15 billion annually, catalog shopping accounts for an additional $15 billion, music CD sales another $20 billion, and telephony more than $200 billion. When we add financial transactions, publishing, computer software, information archives, government services, and education, we see that the impact of convergence is many trillions of dollars of economic activity. As my grandfather used to say, "A trillion here, a trillion there, pretty soon you're talking about real money."

9 INTERACTIVITY
No More Couch Potatoes

"One of the most popular features of America On-line Inc. is its chat rooms, where people can argue, flirt, and generally mouth off ... What's more, AOL's 11 million customers value these services enough that the company was able to raise its prices by 10% in 1998, something car companies have been unable to do."

— *Business Week*, March 23, 1998.

People are naturally "interactive." We love to discuss, argue, and natter with our spouses and friends. Generally we take issue with anything we are *told* to do. We love driving automobiles because we can change lanes, exit the highway, and speed up or slow down as we please. When the sun shines, we put on sunglasses, when it rains, we put up an umbrella, and when a commercial comes on television many of us change the channel. In general, we don't submit to our surroundings; we try to control them.

Interactivity is the ability of a user to change the course of events. It is a contributing trend to the Bagel Effect. Interactivity is fundamentally engaging, communicating, and social.

Interactivity engenders "pull" rather than "push" methodology, that is, it demands that users interrupt the information or entertainment flow, take control of their activity, and *pull* content and services to themselves. The user "drives" the activity. With traditional marketing and broadcasting the supplier *pushes* content and services at the consumer who merely has the power to say no.

Let's Have Intercourse

The most usual form of interactivity is a conversation. A good two-way conversation requires that each speaker also listens to the other and be willing to modify the flow of talk in response to the interventions of the other. Face-to-face conversation is held up as the ideal form of interactivity because the "sender" and "receiver" have access to the greatest quantity and quality of information. The replies are immediate (in real-time) and the communication is in the form of a closed and dedicated circuit. In the field of telecommunications this is called full duplex. You use two channels of information flow — you hear what the other person is saying while you are speaking. This creates a feedback loop that helps form your content.

Intercourse with a Computer

In the 1960s, a flurry of activity in the field of artificial intelligence tried to construct humanlike personalities and interactions within computer software programs. A few efforts successfully simulated social intercourse between humans. Joseph Weizenbaum of MIT's Computer Science Department created "Eliza" with the personality of a Rogerian therapist. Following is a recorded conversation between the Eliza program and a young woman.

Young woman: Men are all alike.

Eliza: In what way?

Young woman: They're always bugging us about something specific or other.

Eliza: Can you think of a specific example?

Young woman: Well, my boyfriend made me come here.

Eliza: Your boyfriend made you come here?

Young woman: He says I'm depressed much of the time.

Eliza: I am sorry to hear you are depressed.

Young woman: It's true. I'm unhappy.

Eliza: Do you think coming here will help you not to be unhappy?

Young woman: I need some help, that much seems certain.

Eliza: What would it mean to you if you got some help?

Young woman: Perhaps I could learn to get along with my mother...

Synthetic personalities can not only converse with people, but with each other. Here's a conversation between Eliza and Parry, a paranoiac personality created by Kenneth Colby of Stanford University Psychiatry Department.

Parry: People get on my nerves sometimes.

Eliza: I am not sure I understand you fully.

Parry: You should pay more attention.

Eliza: Suppose you should pay more attention?

Parry: You're entitled to your opinion.

Eliza: What makes you think I'm entitled to my opinion?

Parry: It bothers me just to be around people.

Eliza: Please go on...

What makes conversation interactive is the ability of the participant to change its course. Although the Eliza simulation was primitive, users found it entertaining and frequently engaging. For some participants the sessions even had therapeutic effect.

Web sites today use synthetic personalities to simulate social and personal conversations. These are visited by netizens who don't always catch on that their conversation isn't with another human. There are sites that feature computer-driven teen-aged girl personalities. Teen-age boys (and some men) spend hours in serious conversation with the synthetic personas, not realizing that their e-mates are ersatz. This illustrates the fundamental and compelling interest people have in being interactive.

Branching

The key to the interactive process is branching. Branching allows a participant to change the flow of events by making a choice. Each choice leads to a different path or branch. Teachers trying to cover a set lesson plan understand the strong tendency students have to stray from the topic at hand and branch into side topics of personal interest. Branching is, in fact, a characteristic of human intelligence. We constantly gather environmental evidence, create hypotheses, and test these against new information and environments.

Most games are interactive and rely heavily on branching. The childhood game of Twenty Questions is engaging because each question leads to a new branch of questioning. Each card that a poker player picks up leads to new branches of possibilities and statistical analyses. Board games like Scrabble and Monopoly keep our attention because every play provides new information and opportunity branches that require careful consideration.

Branching and Bagels

Branching is an activity that puts control in the hands of the user. It contributes directly to the Bagel Effect, as does interactivity in general. As the user gains more freedom of action and as the provider loses the ability to control the process, power flows to the edge of the system. The emergence of the Bagel Effect has been supported by the rise of interactivity, and the rise of interactivity is directly related to appliances with inter-active capability. Chief among these is the computer.

Branching and Computers

Computer microprocessors are fundamentally branching machines. In a sense they are just large aggregations of switches. It is therefore natural that computer programming languages have high capability for branching, for giving users interactive control.

The simplest type of branching code reads like this:

IF <condition that must be fulfilled>

THEN GO TO <address of the branch>

Most computer languages add the capability of random branching so that the user can have a different experience each time the program is run.

IF <condition that must be fulfilled>

THEN GO TO <randomly generated address>

It's not surprising then that the most numerous and commer-cially successful interactive products are computer games, given their fundamentally interactive nature. Even the early and primitive arcade games like *PONG* allow the user to manipulate the outcome of the game. In this case the user moves an object (a paddle) on a video screen as a ball bounces towards it. In computer games, the user interacts with a com-puter-generated environment using a mouse, joystick, rolling ball, trackpad, or other input device.

When we think of computer games we often think of action games, and these remain the most popular with teen-aged boys. But many other interactive games are gaining populari-ty. High on the list are simulations. These range from *SimCity*, in which the player gets to design a city, to Tamagotchi, the virtual pets in the form of tiny computer toys that youngsters must feed and care for lest they get sick and die.

The Power of Play

The Interactive games are so attractive and popular because they give the player power and control over a simulated world. In the real world, it is less likely that the player has such power to control the outcome of his or her pursuits.

The attraction of computer games for kids is easily understood from the child's perspective. Children are among the world's least powerful groups in our society. They lack power because of their diminutive size and lack of experience. They have to do what their parents and teachers tell them to. When they are given the opportunity to play computer games, in which they have expanded powers and can actually best their opponent, the attraction is mesmerizing. How many situations can a six-year-old actually control? How many adversaries can he overcome in the real world?

The arcade game *Pacman,* and its successor *Ms. Pacman,* has a substantial audience of girls and women because it's based on gathering, a traditional female activity. Male-oriented games tend to the primary theme of hunting. Companies are beginning to take advantage of both female and adult game markets that have not yet been tapped. Traditional interest themes for girls and women center on social interactions and secret information (gossip). These are beginning to encroach on typical male themes.

Hyperlinks

When you're playing a game or figuring out a strategy in the real world, all your available branches are not generally presented to you. A new technology called hyperlinking facilitates branching in a manner that is both intuitive and very powerful. Hyperlinks are simply words or images in a document highlighted in a distinctive manner — sometimes with underlining, color, or use of a different type style. The reader may use these hyperlinks to branch to a new page of text, illustration, sound, video, or application, usually by clicking on or pointing at the hyperlink. There is considerable thought given to which links are embedded, where they appear on the display device, and which actions take place when the user interacts.

Hyperlinks are the underlying principle behind the World Wide Web, that portion of the Internet that we access using a browser. This simple technology has resulted in the explosion of Internet pages filled with images, animations, movies, and fancy text.

Programmers can now place hyperlinks that are embedded in moving images as well as text. You can click on the logo of an advertiser, an image of Mars, or an animation of a human heart in action to link you to related content.

For instance, a Web page author might offer you several musical selections that you choose from by clicking on a graphic image using your computer mouse. Clicking on the button invisibly transfers activity to another Web page, which may be located half a world away, where a music file begins downloading to your computer. Within your computer, if you don't already have a music-player software application, a message may go out to yet another Internet site that will automatically download the required music-player to your computer. All the page author does is embed (type in) the addresses of the music file and music-player application. From the user's perspective, there is a seamless flow of activity that results in a satisfying linked operation.

Links allow a programmer to control the interactive flow. They are important bridges between a linear flow controlled by an author, and independent action controlled solely by a user. This cooperative unveiling of content flow, controlled by an author when he or she embeds the links, and controlled by the user when a branching choice is made, is at the heart of the new interactive paradigm. Most systems that exhibit the Bagel Effect put more control at the system edge, but not all.

Interactivity at its core mirrors the social and cooperative nature of people when they have a dialog, but the new technology allows the dialog to be mediated by networks and technology, and be displaced in time (as with e-mail). We can think of hyperlinking as a free-form conversation between the Web page author and the user.

Interactive Media

The term *interactive media* refers to technologies that allow a user to change the course of events in a story, game, reference work, or other content. Although there have been some interesting experiments in interactive theater and cinema, the great majority of interactive media works produced use new media — computer disks, videodiscs, CD-ROMs or Internet technologies — to deliver interactive works.

Fully interactive media allow the sender and receiver (creator and user) roles to be interchanged. Each one is free to respond to the other in a manner that can change the course of the session. Interactive media always include either two communications channels like a telephone or a single reversible channel like a push-to-talk intercom. The telephone system is said to be symmetrical because each person in the conversation has the same amount of bandwidth for listening or talking.

Interactive appliances began with text only, then developed to include images and sounds, and now deliver moving images and animations. As the amount of sensory information increases in the interactive flow the mediated communication more closely approaches a live communication.

Videophones

The videophone is one example of an interactive appliance that has evolved in its capabilities. Until recently these devices were limited by poor technology — low bandwidth — so that the transmitted images exhibited jerky movement, poor audio quality, and very little peripheral view. Advances in network speed and in our understanding of perceptually relevant information are resulting in video-presence — a term coined to indicate a much higher degree of reality than possible in a simple audio-video connection.

Videophones and video-presence will begin to play a major role in the early twenty-first century. Because they are interactive they are consistent with the Bagel Effect and will likely be the dominant conversation technology in the coming decades. Dick Tracy was just a bit ahead of his time.

Avatars and Role-Playing

Interactivity itself is branching into new areas that may soon become mainstream. One of these is the avatar — a cyber-surrogate or alter ego for the user whose representation appears on another user's terminal. In effect, the user creates a role for his or her avatar, giving it whatever personality, traits, and capabilities he or she wishes. The avatar appears on the screen as a face or icon, photograph, or other graphical image, and may carry additional information and sensory clues such as sound effects or a human voice.

Role-playing has become highly popular, with many board games, computer games, and Internet sites available. These games allow the player to assume powers and attributes that affect his or her chance of success in the game. In addition to physical traits, attributes may include magical powers and multiple lives.

The Palace is one of the most popular Internet chat applications. This application creates an architectural and visual space — The Palace — and users take their avatars through its rooms by moving a mouse or other input device. Visitors to The Palace, who may be scattered around the globe, see and can socialize with each other's avatars roaming through the halls, and can also read any text other users are typing — a form of e-conversation.

฿A฿GEL ฿ITS

Shy men sometimes portray themselves using an avatar with bravado and machismo, while circumspect women may wish to take on the image of a sexy vamp. Gender flipping in role-playing is not uncommon. In fact, one of the attractions of avatars is that your proxy can behave in a manner that might feel uncomfortable in real life.

Bob's Your Uncle

A few years back Microsoft heralded a function built into its new Windows operating system, an avatar of the computer itself — Bob. They hoped that this anthropomorphism of the computer would become a friend and agent to users and that they would be more likely to ask him for assistance. But Bob bombed in the marketplace, perhaps because his computerized voice irritated many users.

Microsoft has reworked the concept of Bob in their new operating systems. He is now a trouble-shooter and has lost some of his simulated human characteristics while increasing his interactive capabilities. No longer a simulated person, this new computer assistant continually monitors your activities and when they match a pattern indicating a problem, it interrupts your session with a beep and suggests help options that are sensitive to the context of your work. This is a more comfortable avatar for a computer, a digital assistant rather than a human persona.

Experts Said People Wouldn't Interact

Until the World Wide Web proved otherwise, experts held that people didn't want to be interactive in their leisure time. For more than forty years it's been the accepted truth that we want to sit back, relax, and experience what others have programmed for us. Asking an audience to participate was tantamount to asking them to turn the program off.

That belief led to pronouncements as recent as 1995 that the Internet and World Wide Web would not catch on because they were too interactive and demanded too much input from users.

Figure 9.1 - Interactive Fried Potato

In 1992 when CulTech Research Centre was founded, we planned our research projects based on the then-unarticulated principles of the Bagel Effect. My colleagues and I felt certain that computers and the Internet would become mass-market phenomena even as analysts around the world disagreed heartily. Broadcast and telecommunications executives were fixated on the 500-television-channel universe as the route to the Information Society of the twenty-first century. They envisaged the future as not much different from the present, there'd just be more of it — more choices of linear programming, in which the user must accept the producer's content or change channels.

CulTech believed that people have a natural predilection for interfering with and controlling their environment, and that since computers and the World Wide Web are essentially interactive, they would likely succeed.

Storytelling is Naturally Interactive

When Norman Jewison, well known Hollywood film director and founder of the Canadian Film Centre, met Nicholas Negroponte, the Media Lab's director and author of *Being*

Digital, they launched into a discussion about the use of digital technology in films. Norman's conversation topper was simply, "I'm just telling a story ... digital technology is just another tool to help me accomplish that."

The most natural form of storytelling is interactive. Anyone with a younger sibling or a child knows that children have an insatiable appetite for stories. Their imagination prompts them to interrupt the story, to demand that the name of a character be changed, to add dwarves to the Cinderella story, or perhaps to change the ending of Red Riding Hood so that the wolf is friendly. Storytelling is, after all, an oral tradition in which tellers react to their audience and surroundings by elaborating certain story elements and eliminating others.

Linear Flow

Following is a simple flow chart of a traditional dramatic story line. The writer sets up the conflict, characters, and setting, then proceeds to add plot points that ultimately build to a climax and finally a resolution of the conflict.

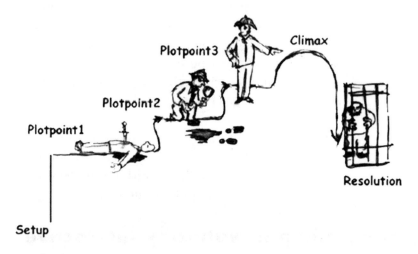

Figure 9.2 - Linear Flow Chart

Interactive Flow

It's more difficult to diagram the flow of interactive story-telling. Ira Nyman, a non-linear author who led a discussion at Interactive '96, a conference for artists and creators, explained it thus: "Mary had a little lamb. Its fleece was white as snow. And everywhere that Mary went ... Pick one of the following choices."

Running time for an interactive story depends on which story paths the user chooses, the number of branching options, and where the branching takes place. Early branching requires more story lines than late branching. The following illustrates the difference between running length and story length for an interactive work:

Two writers are each asked to create a simple interactive story for a computer kiosk in a mall. Each story is to have three parts, a set beginning, a choice of middle parts, and a set ending. Each part will run one minute and will occupy a single page of script. One writer constructs a beginning scene 1, an ending scene 3, and two options for the middle, scene 2a and scene 2b. The second writer also constructs a single beginning scene 1 and ending scene 3, but allows for ten versions of the middle parts, scenes 2a, 2b, 2c, 2d, 2e, 2f, 2g, 2h, 2i, 2j. The running time for both works is three minutes, but one writer has written four pages of script while the second writer has written twelve pages of script.

In the flowchart on the following page there is a set scene #1 at the beginning from which the user can choose three paths. Each of these paths returns the user to scene #5, which all users will see. From here there are three new choices which themselves branch in numerous ways. In the case of scene #9 the narrative returns to scene #5, in the other cases the story moves on. This example shows two possible endings, scene #23, and scene #24.

Following is a typical flow chart for an interactive story.

Figure 9.3 - Interactive Flowchart

Every form of interactive content, ranging from arcade-style games to educational courses, requires this type of interactive flow chart in order to understand how the user may navigate the content.

Authors Lose Control

Interactivity takes control away from authors, composers, playwrights, filmmakers, directors, and producers. The considerable skills they have honed over many long years that enable them to create linear content with cohesion and a sense of climax are tossed to the winds as soon as they let the user control the flow. These creators are being pulled kicking and screaming into the new age of interactivity because users are showing increasingly greater preference for these types of works.

This is a very difficult time for the television and radio industries. Some argue that broadcasting is all about flow.

Frequently the flow is what differentiates one channel from another since the programs tend to be very similar. When the flow-control is given to the audience, how can broadcasters continue to justify their jobs?

Interactive Communities

The next century will see an explosion of a new style of community enabled by digital connectivity. Its emergence will be as significant as the explosion of suburbs was when automobiles were introduced. Interactive communities give residents much greater input into their local governments, schools, and suppliers. Communities are being built throughout the world with digital connectivity that will allow for much greater interactivity among the residents than we have today.

One such planned community will be in Malaysia where Prime Minister YAB Dato' Seri Dr. Mahathir bin Mohamad is leading a project he hopes will vault Malaysia ahead of other developing nations in economic growth and quality of life. His goal is no less than wiring an entire region with digital interactivity in all the homes, schools, and businesses. The target timetable for transforming the country is the year 2020.

Intercom Ontario

In Canada, a Newmarket, Ontario community called Stonehaven West has been wired for interactivity and is the first such community anywhere in the world to deliver a wide range of interactive content. One of the first and most important research results is that these people are much more social than in other communities. Residents report that they get to know their neighbors more quickly than in other neighborhoods where they have lived. They also get to know more of them. A few weeks after the first residents were connected, they requested a directory of their neighbors' e-mail and videophone addresses. Residents were asked permission before their addresses were placed in the neighborhood directory and most gave it. Shortly thereafter the residents began e-mailing invitations to barbecues and other community events that brought them into face-to-face conversation.

Previous research demonstrated that videophones are most effective after the parties to the conversation have already met face-to-face and established a rapport. Here we see the reverse: people meet first electronically and then use the electronic communication to set up face-to-face communications.

Residents soon found that they had much greater power and leverage with local authorities, schools, and even with the real estate developer because they could exchange views and bring cohesive and united arguments forward to improve the quality of their community.

Making Music

Interactive networks will bring many new and exciting activities. In 1995, my band Lighthouse did a performance at the closing ceremonies of the international Smart Cities Conference, in which half of us (guitar, keyboard, bass, drums, singer) were at the Toronto Conference Centre and the other half (trumpet, two saxophones, trombone, keyboard, and singer) were twenty kilometers distant at Centennial College. At each location there was a life-sized image on stage of the remote players. The technological feat was accomplished by collaboration between Rogers Cable TV and Bell Canada.

Although the purpose of the performance was entertainment and research, it opened the door to a future in which we will have interactive access to many activities from our homes.

BAGEL BITS

A young musician living in a rural area might not have access to a good local teacher, but using networked video-presence could take regular violin lessons, say, with a teacher in nearby city, or play in a string quartet with other musicians from around the globe.

A year later at the InterActive '96 conference, technology had improved enough that I was able to telepresence four locations — The Centre for Innovation in Technology in Montreal, the Bamboo Club in Toronto (where a party was in full force), the Bravo! television studios, and the Fine Arts Broadcast Centre at York University. This time I put together a jazz band with the drummer and bass player in Montreal, the sax and trumpet at the Bamboo, the guitar player at York University, and myself at a grand piano at the Bravo! TV studios. We each had a monitor that displayed the images of all locations onto a single screen.

Megatrend Streams

We've shown how downsizing, decentralization, deregulation, digitization, convergence, and interactivity have combined to produce the megatrend I call the Bagel Effect. The next section will demonstrate how these component trends gained much more impact and synchronization as a result of the chance occurrence of two events of global importance.

PART 3
CATALYSTS

Central Economies Fall, Digital Networks Rise

The combined effects of downsizing, decentralization, deregulation, digitization, convergence, and interactivity would have undoubtedly resulted in a Bagel Effect of significant proportions. Yet each individual trend had its own timetable with a different starting point, peaks, and valleys. For instance, digitization began changing products and processes almost two decades before interactivity had a significant impact on our lives.

Although we were all exposed to these contributing trends in the media, prior to the '90s it was difficult to measure their collective importance. To make a dent in our collective awareness, they needed simple, unifying images. Two catalytic events took place near the close of the twentieth century which provided such unity and brought all six trends into synchronization.

Each was a pivotal event that crossed national and cultural boundaries. Each caught the attention of people throughout the world with its metaphoric meaning. They were:

- The Fall of Communism
- The Rise of the Internet

These events were catalysts for the Bagel Effect and increased its visibility and impact. They elevated the Bagel Effect to a dominant force driving change at the turn of the millennium.

10 FALL OF COMMUNISM

Controlled Economies Lose to Free Markets

"Over the last years we have seen a World Wide shift away from government ownership and regulated monopolies towards privatization and competition. From Armenia, which announced it would soon be completing its process of privatization, to Zimbabwe ... virtually all countries have been struggling with the need to redesign basic national structures..."

— Hudsen Janish, Faculty of Law, University of Toronto.

Growing up in the creampuff years was very different than today. The pervasive underlying theme was the Cold War. Families built fallout shelters stocked with food and guns so that when the Russians attacked North America with nuclear weapons they could protect themselves from the blast and also from their neighbors.

The Soviets intoned, "We will bury you... Free enterprise will end up on the scrap heap of history." The American and Canadian governments gave credence to Soviet boasts of military and scientific superiority because it allowed them to raise taxes and spend trillions on military and industrial programs which created jobs and fired nationalist feelings. The Cuban Missile Crisis brought the reality of the Soviet threat home with images of Soviet missile bases a few dozens miles off the North American coast.

Central Planning

The hallmark of the Soviet system was central economic planning, a series of five-year plans that dictated every aspect of the economy. A central planning committee in the ministry of agriculture would specify how many farmers could farm and what they could grow. Never mind that Nature didn't take direction from the committee and thwarted the crop projections with unpredictable weather. Never mind that the committee members determined what food would be available to eat without regard for what the people might like to eat. Never mind that all the good quality food "fell off" the supply trucks and ended up in local larders. And never mind that bureaucrats, eager to meet their targets, set unrealistic quotas for farmers who had no incentives to meet them.

In retrospect, the folly of central planning seems obvious, but in those days, the majority of the countries in the world believed that the communist economic structure would succeed as the new world order. It would be imposed first in the underdeveloped countries and ultimately in the developed world as well.

I visited Poland when the country was in the last throes of its centrally planned economy. After a meal at a Polish restaurant, the waiter suggested that I pay for it in American dollars. All tourists knew that there was a tremendous black-market demand for currency and that we shouldn't exchange our money on the streets, but this was just a case of paying for dinner. It was obvious, however, that the price in dollars was much lower than the cost of dinner. I watched the waiters carefully and realized that they were pocketing the American money and not turning it in to the cashier.

"How can they get away with this?" I wondered. "Surely someone will notice that the income from customers is not enough to cover the cost of the food!" A few days later a Polish cab driver explained it to me. In the Soviet economy there was no concept of profit and loss — these were seen as capitalist constructs. Here the ministry of agriculture would send food to the restaurant and the ministry of tourism would take the receipts. The two ministries would never reconcile their books, so the waiters could pocket most of the customers' payments without anyone noticing.

Although we knew that the Soviets were our enemies and although we parroted our catechism of communist evils, Western democracies nonetheless adopted many of the artifacts of centrally planned governments. Unemployment Insurance and the Canada Pension Plan are watered-down versions of socialist-style programs. The size of our own governments grew enormously in this period of anti-Communist focus, both in size and in power.

When a social or economic problem cropped up, a new government program was inaugurated to solve it. Very few government programs were ever wound down. The result was huge bureaucracies vested in the public service, which became the largest employers in North America. So long as our economies were in long-term expansion these commensurate expansions of government seemed reasonable.

Socialism and Marxism at Home

We enshrined free enterprise at home, but most of us believed that the socialist model worked better for poor and emerging countries. Many believed that socialism could work for us as well, if we wouldn't be so selfish about accumulating wealth. Sweden was frequently paraded as an example of successful socialism in a democratic context.

University campuses were a haven for Marxist thinking. Many courses deconstructed twentieth century events from a Marxist perspective. The reaction against American involvement in Viet Nam helped align student thinking with left-leaning organizations.

Central regulation was welcomed by many large industries. In Canada, the airlines, telephone companies, broadcasters, gas and oil producers welcomed government regulation because it protected their markets from competition.

And the Walls Came Tumbling Down

Suddenly, the Soviet system collapsed, and the shock was immense. Unless you lived through it, you couldn't imagine the powerful impact of the Berlin Wall falling. As it crumbled, the image of Communism and the strong centrally controlled state crumbled with it. We gasped and spoke about the events that were transpiring. "Yes. I knew it all along. It had to collapse under its own weight. Communism could never work. You can never restrain free will. People need financial incentives to work..."

The Soviet Union imploded and quickly splintered into the component countries that had existed before Communism. Television networks broadcast the toppling of statues of Lenin and other Communist heroes. The bubble had burst. Decentralization and deregulation had gained an incredibly strong metaphoric image that will remain with us for the rest of our lives.

Developing World

When the Soviet Union collapsed, worldwide communism lacked an ideological headquarters and also lost its main financier. In the Middle East, Far East, Africa, South America, and the Caribbean, developing countries that had relied on economic support from the Soviet Union suddenly found themselves out of cash. There's nothing like an empty belly to encourage a change in politics and economics. One by one, the countries that had been in the Soviet economic sphere of central planning jumped into the free enterprise camp. Some slowly, some more quickly, but without the center itself — the Soviet Union — enthusiasm for the idea faded quickly.

New Freedoms

The Soviet political system was a single party that restrained freedom and choice. With the breakdown of this system came the new political realities of multi-party democracy, free markets, freedom of assembly, freedom of expression, and so on. As these Bagel Effect indicators became evident, so did their extreme manifestations, chaos and anarchy. Russia and the other component countries of the old Communist Bloc continue to struggle with the instability of the Freedom Pendulum as it rests momentarily at its extreme position until it begins to swing back towards greater security and order.

Governments Conform to Bagel Effect

Governments everywhere are moving away from centralization, bureaucracy, and regulation, and towards the Bagel Effect. Federal governments are becoming smaller, ceding power to state and provincial governments. These in turn have been downloading many of their programs and powers to local municipalities. Ultimately, ordinary citizens are gaining more power than ever before.

The other side of empowerment is responsibility, and with each divesting of power from the center outwards, there is a concomitant responsibility placed on citizens to look after themselves and each other. For many, these new found obligations are seen as burdens. The central safety nets are being withdrawn, making life riskier for those who live in a precarious balance. On the other hand, it can be argued that the family is being strengthened as it re-emerges as the caregiving unit for the old, sick, and poor.

All Parties Cut Bureaucracy

The impact of the Fall of Communism and its attendant lesson to eliminate bureaucracy has been so powerful as to affect all political parties, on the left as well as the right. In the early 1990s in Ontario, New Democratic Premier Bob Rae began to downsize the civil service with the result that his ideological base of union supporters deserted him. The handwriting was on the wall, however, and politicians from all sides of the aisle could read it.

11 THE RISE OF THE INTERNET
A Perfect Bagel

"The functionality of the Internet has been pushed to the edges — it is a stupid network as opposed to the telephone network, which is much smarter but has stupid appliances (telephones) at its edges. As a result, one could change the protocol of the Internet (TCP) without changing its component routers while the telephone network cannot be changed without discarding its essential components."

— Dr. David Clark of MIT's Laboratory for Computer Science in his book, *Design and Operation of the Internet*

The Internet is a perfect bagel. This anarchic virtual network of networks has no center. It is an example of all power and control shifted to the edges of a system — to the users at their computer appliances. It is unusual to see anarchic human-built systems since people control their environment whenever they can. We spend a considerable portion of our lives trying to keep it all together, imposing human order on the natural disorderly force (entropy) of the universe.

The Internet may be the human system most closely resembling a bagel. Although it is huge and extraordinarily complex, it has no central administration. This was not an accident. The same Cold War that hastened the downfall of the Communist empire accounted for the formation of the Internet.

Government, corporations, and universities have funded the Internet while at the same time freeing it from their control. One of the reasons that the Internet has been a catalyst for the Bagel Effect is that it was formed at a time when big business and government tightly controlled telecommunications. End users jumped from having no telecommunications freedom at all to being totally in control of the Internet.

Baking a Perfect Bagel

The folks who invented the Internet were computer scientists at the Massachusetts Institute of Technology, but their patron saint was the United States Department of Defense. In 1969, the U.S. Defense Department commissioned ARPANET, the predecessor to the Internet. They charged scientists with creating a communications system that could withstand the trauma of a surprise nuclear attack from the Soviet Union so that the president, cabinet, and military leaders could coordinate a counterattack from their secure bunkers. In the 1970s this was serious stuff. With Soviet nuclear missiles aimed at strategic American locations, and spies ferreting out the location of strategic American targets, the network inventors had to come up with a novel solution.

They assumed the location of the nerve center could not be kept secret, so the decision was made to design a communications system that had no administrative center at all. The brilliant solution was to have a network with no fixed signal path, so that if one or more sections were destroyed, the signals would change routes to arrive at their destinations unharmed. Unlike the telephone network, which switches signals onto physical wires in known locations, the Internet would be a virtual network, and no one would ever know what path a signal took to reach its destination.

One cannot imagine that this project would have been funded except in the name of national security. After all, governments are elected to impose and preserve order, while this new technology was disorderly by design. The Internet's unusual structure resembles a many-tentacled organism whose arms are in communication with each other but without a head or a heart. If any portion of the network is destroyed, data and communications are automatically rerouted. We speak of it as self-healing.

In 1974, Bob Kahn and Vince Cerf published a paper specifying the Internet Protocol standard that would define the Internet but it wasn't until 1982 that the Defense Department formally established TCP/IP as the standard networking protocol. The power of this protocol was so great that within just two years there were more than one thousand host computers connected to the Internet, and five years later, there were more than one hundred thousand.

Although the Internet began as a communications and research network, it began to encompass commercial transactions in 1991, as businesses awoke to the opportunities afforded by inexpensive global connectivity.

In 1992, scientists working at CERN, the European laboratory for particle physics, invented the World Wide Web — that part of the Internet that most people use today. They wanted to make the Internet easier to use, so they invented a new computer language, HTML (see Chapter 9, Interactivity) which added a new capacity for controlling images and sounds as well as text. To experience these World Wide Web pages you need a browser — an application that interprets the HTML and combines the images, sounds and text into a single document displayed on a computer monitor.

With the creation of the World Wide Web, the potential of the Internet went through the roof. Instead of limiting the Internet audience to computer enthusiasts, the concept was so powerful that it drove non-computer-users to buy their first computer, just to get onto the Web. Within a year of the World Wide Web's creation, American President Bill Clinton and Vice President Al Gore had public e-mail addresses.

By 1995, it was clear that the scope of the Net and the Web had far outgrown the initial vision of a military-sponsored network for government and research institutions. Traffic was turned over to commercial service providers who now fund its backbone operations. They earn revenue from Internet access providers who in turn charge users a monthly fee.

The Internet may be compared to the world-wide postal system in which each participating country manages its own postal service. Each user has a unique address, each local postal unit its own postal code. The Internet electronics read the address on each information packet and route it along a path to its ultimate destination.

In 1996, there were more than twelve million connected computers (hosts) on the Internet and more than five hundred thousand Web sites. By February 1998, there were thirty million connected computers in 240 countries and territories. The number of users was estimated at sixty million, since several users frequently share a computer. By the year 2000, Internet providers expect about two hundred million users with about 60% of these in North America.

A Disorganized System

The biggest problem for Internet users is that the information system is not organized, so it can be tough to find what you're looking for. As a result the most useful and popular Internet application is the search engine. Web sites such as Yahoo! and Excite are among the most visited areas on the Internet because they allow users to search for sites of interest by typing topics, names, or even scraps of information. The search engine returns an almost instant list of corresponding sites. Search sites continually employ Web crawlers — software that explores the entire Internet, automatically creating electronic text indexes, which are used for retrieving search data.

Information Superhighway

Early in his term as U.S. Vice President, Al Gore became a great champion for what he called the Information Superhighway. The term had been kicking around elsewhere, but Gore seized on the metaphor because his father, Senator Albert Gore Sr., had been the author of the American interstate superhighway legislation. It was a natural for the Veep to seek a place in history as the author of his generation's digital superhighway system.

Unlike physical highways where the user is in a vehicle spending significant time and energy navigating an asphalt-and-concrete infrastructure, digital networks create virtual paths from here to there that are traversed almost instantly. In true Bagel style, they place less importance on the traveling and more on the activities on the outer edges of the infrastructure.

The Infoway

The term Information Superhighway was quickly contracted to Infoway, much quicker to say and write, and without the metaphoric baggage of automobiles and trucks. The Infoway is not yet a mature market, either in Canada or on a global basis. It should not be thought of as a single economic sector since it cuts across many sectors. Rather, it is a quickly evolving system that presents two particular opportunities:

- An electronic marketplace unrestricted by territorial boundaries, a boon for local content suppliers;
- A level playing field among market participants, with great opportunities for new players.

More Virtual Travel

A profound change brought about by the Infoway is that we will travel much less frequently to where goods and services are. These can be delivered either directly through the digital network or transacted on the network and delivered by snail-mail (mail or courier). This is taking some stress off the physical infrastructure, as SOHOs — small office, home office — and teleworkers conduct their business lives at home. Road-building materials (petroleum, concrete), cars and trucks (steel, aluminum, rubber) and community planning are being affected, as people switch from physical roads to virtual info-roads. Many activities that today require that you go to a school, library, store, doctor's office, cinema, or bank will be available at home without the need for physical travel.

Governments Backing Off

In North America, governments focusing on budget deficits have retreated from infrastructure funding. But, as the private sector is asked to deliver a larger share of this infrastructure, it is also demanding a larger role. Since companies have an obligation to bring profits to their shareholders, there is a shift in focus from providing maximum citizen benefits to providing maximum shareholder benefits.

Governments fund most of the highway infrastructure in North America and it's possible to travel to most places without paying a toll. In the case of digital infrastructures we have a system where tolls are the norm and citizens are stratified into info-enabled and info-disabled. Paradoxically, the groups that are economically disadvantaged have much to gain from Infoways, because it can bring them training, education, job placement, and health counseling. Those who live in remote areas have even more to gain from the increased access to remote services.

Early Communications Infrastructure

The transcontinental railway was the first national transportation system constructed in Canada. It had many parallels to today's Infoways, providing essential connectivity for the development of Canada as a nation. Like our new Infoways it caused major changes in where people lived, how they communicated, how they traveled, how their businesses operated, and even what kinds of entertainment they had. Modern circuses, for example, developed as a direct consequence of rail travel.

The railways provided a new distribution network that caught the imagination of the public. They spawned many new businesses, such as catalog shopping, which became popular because goods could be delivered quickly. The biggest problem the railway builders had to face was the cost of the infrastructure. The problem then, like now, was that there was not enough business at the start to pay for the roadbeds and stations.

C.D. Howe realized it was necessary to create destinations for travelers in order to attract traffic. His vision produced the Canadian Pacific and Canadian National hotel chains. The railroad owners built these destinations to entice tourists and business people to travel on the new infrastructure. The government assisted by establishing national parks like Banff and Lake Louise to entice travelers to come along the new routes.

Infoways similarly lack enough desirable destinations to generate profitable commercial traffic. Like the railway builders, infrastructure providers such as telcos are being pulled into the business of creating destinations. For digital networks, the destinations are applications and content instead of bricks and mortar, but the implications are the same and the same dilemma exists. How do you pay for Infoway infrastructure before there's a business model to support it? And how can content creators make a case for creating the destinations until there's an infrastructure in place to distribute their works and pay for them?

The early days of rail travel were plagued with highwaymen like Jesse James who took advantage of the new system's lack of security to steal from companies and travelers who used it. The same holds true of the Internet, although cyber-bandits don't have to risk their lives. It took many years to bring law, order, and regulation to the railways and it will take some time to do the same for the Infoway. Nonetheless, a combination of technology-based protection schemes and new copyright legislation is beginning to make the Infoway at least as secure as our physical distribution systems.

Intranets

Since the Internet is such a hit, it is not surprising that organizations would want to piggy-back on its success by using the same protocols and equipment for private networks. A private network is called an intranet. Intranets are simply corporate, government, university, or even personal networks that are compatible with the Internet.

They differ from the Internet because they have administration, most notably firewalls — devices that control access to and from the intranet. Intranet users have access to each other and to services within the private network, but the firewall restricts traffic to and from the Internet.

If the term extranet crops up, don't panic. These are simply intranets that have been extended outside the local campus of an institution or company. In the case of corporate intranets, network administrators may wish to limit many types of Internet access. A common one is e-mail, which may be secure on a private intranet but not secure on the Internet. Corporations do not wish to have their private data subjected to prying eyes, so they frequently block Internet mail from inter-operating with their corporate e-mail system.

BAGEL BITS

America On-line is a large commercial intranet. When you pay your monthly content fee you get access to private AOL Web sites and services available only to subscribers. AOL's firewall prevents Internet users from accessing AOL content, although it has been configured to allow AOL customers to access Internet Web sites. This is known as a semi-permeable firewall.

E-mail

The most popular Internet application from its inception has been e-mail. E-mail allows a user to send messages to any other user, like regular mail. In addition, e-mail allows a user to send messages to many other users (broadcast) and to attach files, send copies of messages to others, and perform computer storage and search functions. Once people start using e-mail, it's difficult for them to do without it. It is the epitome of a Bagel service: no central administration; power and control with individual users at the edges of the system; open and democratic access.

Netiquette

Although it lacks central administration, the Internet has developed a consensus system of management known simply as netiquette — short for network etiquette. Service providers generally publish documents for clients relating to suggested netiquette and have voluntary subscriber codes of conduct. For example, some actions prohibited in AOL's On-line Conduct guide are:

- Offensive Communications — vulgar, abusive or hateful language;
- Harassment — causing distress, embarrassment, unwanted attention, or other discomfort to another user;

- Personal attacks — based on race, national origin, ethnicity, religion, gender, sexual orientation, disablement or other such affiliation;
- Scrolling — repeatedly entering a carriage return having a disruptive effect on other users;
- Impersonation — portrayal of another person or entity;
- Room Disruption — interfering with the normal flow of dialogue in a chat room;
- Chain Letters — junk mail and pyramid schemes.

Novices who break the netiquettes are liable to receive barrages of unwanted mail — spam — and other network harassment from voluntary network vigilantes.

Internet Fax

Currently, Fortune 500 companies each spend about $15 million a year on fax service. Now that most of the business world is on the Internet, it has become a viable alternative to telephone lines for sending faxes. The bottom line is excellent — there are no long-distance charges. Forty percent of all international telephone calls are fax-related and about 5% of this business is expected to quickly migrate to the Internet by 1999 — that's more than $1 billion. Because a fax message is digital, and can withstand the small momentary interruptions that the Internet is prone to, it is an ideal candidate for moving to the new network.

Internet Telephony

Technical breakthroughs are bringing the feasibility of using the Internet telephony closer to reality. Bill St. Arnaud of CANARIE reports that "bandwidth costing more than $5,000 a month to deliver in January 1998 may cost .... as little as $50 a month before the end of 1999." As this book is being written, the best guess is that telephone service could be provided using Internet infrastructures at one-tenth the price of using the switched telephone networks.

Although the technical problems of delivering high-quality voice telephony over the Internet are more difficult to solve than the problems of bringing fax service to the Net, they are nonetheless solvable. By the year 2000, there will be significant cannibalization of telephone traffic by the Internet.

The multi-trillion-dollar global telecommunications industry is at stake. Companies are spending billions to build a new Internet-like infrastructure with enormous capacity that is much cheaper to deploy than traditional telephone networks.

Wireless Internet

Wireless Internet technologies are starting to come on-line. Seven new Internet-in-the-sky systems will be operational in the early years of the twenty-first century and these will make the Internet available in every nook and cranny of the globe, even in places that don't currently have telephones. The result will be an Internet that subsumes the power and reach of traditional telephone networks.

Fast Internet

The biggest complaint about the Internet is that it is too slow. Originally designed for text, it has been unable to meet the demands of Web sites offering graphics, sound and video, which require much greater bandwidth than text. The modems that connect consumers to the Internet have not increased their capacity as quickly as the increased data flow, leading to long delays in many situations.

With users clammoring for faster Internet, cable and telephone companies have been scrambling to provide solutions. For cable television companies, the solution is to hive off a portion of the enormous bandwidth available to coaxial cables (see Chapter 14, Television) and dedicate it to delivering Internet services. The devices that do this are called cable modems. They typically deliver more than ten times the speed of a normal modem working on a telephone line. Unfortunately, the cable television infrastructure was not designed to accept signals from users, so cable companies have to upgrade their facilities in order to deliver the fast Internet service, which requires that users have interactive two-way communication with Web sites.

For telephone companies, the technical problems are tougher because their copper wires were designed to carry low-bandwidth voice, not high-bandwidth television signals. Consequently, the technical solutions are more expensive. One solution is to replace the copper telephone wires to each home with coaxial cable, like cable TV wires. Another is to use a fancier modem to increase the speed of Internet service. The second solution is cheaper, but the modem signals can't travel very far in telephone wires before they are degraded, so telcos have to place new equipment closer to users' homes than their central offices. For either solution, the cost of providing fast Internet service is higher for the telcos than it is for cable television companies (see Chapter 17, Telephony).

Big Money?

To date, most companies have not yet figured out how to make big money on the Internet. Microsoft, the company that absolutely dominates the computer software industry, has continually lost money on its Internet ventures. While Bay Street and Wall Street debate whether Netscape or Microsoft will dominate the Internet browser market, other players are developing applications with built-in browsers that could completely bypass the Microsoft and Netscape products.

The Bagel Effect predicts that end users will not want to buy computers, operating systems or applications that force them to access the Internet from a single supplier. This was evident in the early '90s when SONY brought out a Personal Digital Assistant whose utility and feature-set were excellent. Trouble was, it was hardwired for using AT&T and America On-line for Internet access and content providers. Consumers bridled at the thought of having their choices limited, and the product died.

BAGEL BITS

RealMedia is a computer application that plays music and videos over the Internet. It can operate as stand alone software, without an Internet browser. Consequently, the RealMedia application gets to display advertising, not the Microsoft or Netscape browser. By circumventing these access applications, it scoops the ad revenue and destroys the browser business model.

Internet — The Next Generation

Like the pendulum at one extreme of its path, the Internet is in a position of instability, and has already started to swing back towards the center. The first signs are apparent. Credit card companies and other transaction mediators are using encryption and authorization systems on the Internet today. Users must agree to terms and conditions that allow administrators to regulate their access to goods and services. These controls have been grafted onto the Internet and are awkward to use, but they are allowing this anarchic system to impose its own central administration and controls, making it friendly to commerce and regulation.

The proposed next generation of the Internet Protocol will have built-in security mechanisms and will support authentication and secure transactions. An authentication mechanism will ensure that the person identified in the message header did in fact transmit the message and that it has not been tampered with in transit. Privacy, the assurance that only authorized parties can see messages, will be implemented by strong encryption.

The New Internet

The new Internet will be a digital network of networks that is no longer anarchic, chaotic, and free. It will be commerce-friendly with enough bandwidth for television-quality images. It will, in fact, be the Infoway foreseen in the early '90s. Many will bemoan this development and the result will be the bifurcation of the Internet into two interoperable digital networks:

- One will remain true to the intentions and philosophies of the original netizens. It will be public and universally accessible. All content will be free, and it will continue to provide anonymity to users.
- The second will be administered and regulated. Materials deemed offensive, such as kiddy-porn, hate propaganda, and plans for building nuclear bombs, will be restricted from Web sites. The new Net will allow the integration of intellectual property management systems, which will change the way we acquire most of our goods and services.

PART 4
MEDIA

Is the Medium the Message?

Two defining human characteristics are the ability to make tools and to communicate. We communicate information, emotions, and context. When we communicate directly with another person, we include many auditory and visual clues that add information to the message we are trying to convey. We accept that our eyes are receivers of visual information, but we don't usually think about them as transmitting information. Yet the way we look at another person (or don't) when we speak to them can convey more information than the words we speak.

When non-human agents mediate our communications, some of this information is lost. In addition, the medium alters the messages. For example, tribal drums have been used as a medium for communication since prehistory. The messages they communicate are filtered through the limitations of the drums as compared to two people speaking to each other in physical proximity. The drum language contains a much smaller vocabulary than the language spoken by the people sending and receiving the drum messages. The messages can therefore convey only information that can be expressed in the limited language of the drums.

The same holds true for more recent and complex media such as:

- Print
- Records
- Television
- Cinema
- Computers
- Telephones
- New Media

In each case the mediating technology filters the messages and presents them differently than would a live person. Since the media alter messages, and since we are bombarded with increasing numbers of messages through new media, it's no wonder we get a lot of mixed messages.

The following section examines the media we use and explains how they are being influenced by the Bagel Effect megatrend. Digital convergence has reduced the fundamental message unit in all cases to the digital bit and convergence has made these bits available in many media. The result is no less than a fundamental change in how we perceive the world around us and how we are able to communicate our own thoughts and feelings to others.

PRINT
Stop the Presses?

Speech is a natural form of human communication, whereas alphabets and writing are relatively recent accomplishments in the history of humankind. And printing itself is only a few hundred years old. Yet, the printing press arguably has had more impact on our civilization than any other technology invented over the past thousand years. Nonetheless, the age of printing as we know it — the technology of mass-producing copies using type in mechanized printing presses — is nearing its end.

Printing is a creampuff technology. It is a centrally controlled process geared to mass markets as opposed to individual readers. A reader has little control over reading a book or magazine, as compared to reading text on a monitor screen. In print media, the publisher selects the font size, the typeface, the number of columns on a page, the number of words in a column, and the size of a page. These and other aspects of document presentation are routinely controlled by readers on monitor screens.

In addition, the book does not allow for random access to text nor for searching by topic. In fact, after printing was invented it took almost a hundred years to come up with page numbers, one of the few reader-oriented improvements that have been made over time. The Bagel Effect suggests that mass-production printing will diminish in importance, giving way to newer technologies that will move more control to readers.

So, why would I present this document as a book? The answers are simple.

- There is no other medium today that can reach as many readers;
- There is no other medium today that is comfortable for long-form reading;
- As an author, I like to control the presentation of my work.

McLuhan on Print

It is difficult to discuss print without invoking the insights of this century's great media guru Marshall McLuhan. On February 18, 1960, in a letter to David Riesman, he wrote:

> When the globe becomes a single electronic computer ... the fixed point of print culture becomes irrelevant and impossible, no matter how precious. (from *Understanding McLuhan*, CD Rom, Voyager)

McLuhan refers to the concept of printing to a mass market from a single physical location as "irrelevant." As the world becomes networked with computer technology, the physical distribution of printed copies becomes unnecessary and much more costly than just-in-time printing where and when the material is needed. Note that in 1960, when global networks were not even on the drawing boards, McLuhan observed:

> We're moving out of the age of the mass-produced package into the age of the personal and private service.

This nails the Bagel Effect dead-on. McLuhan was speaking about books as mass-produced packages and about photocopying as personal and private services. Moving from centrally controlled information to individually tailored information increases user control, a Bagel Effect.

Print Is Linear

Books are a linear medium. They generally require the reader to start at the beginning and to proceed to the end without interrupting the linear flow of material.

Over the years books have incorporated some mildly interactive elements, such as tables of contents and indexes which give readers some control over the flow of the material, but the very nature of printing (preset pages) prevents significant user interaction.

Is Print Anti-Social?

At the same time, because they remove the reader from conversation, books tend to be anti-social. Reading tends to draw one into a private world rather than a public and social one. Books encourage contemplative reflection, but bookworms tend to cocoon and remove themselves from reality.

There is no doubt that reading books can stimulate thoughts that lead to conversation afterwards, but the same may be said of watching television programs, which are also linear. It's interesting that many who righteously laud the value of print media are the same lot who decry the decadence of television, although the two media share the same essential non-interactive characteristic.

Waiting for the E-Book

The classic first stage of a new technology introduction is an echo of the previous technology. Although most would not realize it, we are now waiting for the perfect e-book. When it arrives, the switch from print to digital text will be very rapid. It's reasonable to expect that this e-book appliance will be invented in the next decade.

Books are mature and user-friendly appliances. And because the pocket book is the most popular format, the e-book's design will likely mimic it. The pocket book fits into a purse or a jacket pocket and is easily held for reading on a bus, train, airplane, or in bed. The closest appliances today are the personal digital organizers, such as the PalmPilot. The problem with using these for reading is that their screens are too small to display enough text, the text is not as legible as it is on a high-contrast printed page, and they lack key features that would make them more useful than books.

The two most-asked-for features in e-books are variable sized text (the over-forties generally want it bigger) and user-defined bookmarks. The ability for users to place bookmarks and comments in electronic text is a major improvement over print media. How many times have you read something and wished you could make note of it, so you could discuss it with a friend, or so you could find it immediately later when you want it?

The e-book will not have content of its own. You will load the book's content when you need it from the nearest infrared or other wireless tap in your home, office, library, or retail store. You will, of course, be able to connect the book to a computer network for wired loading of content, but this seems unnecessarily cumbersome. You will be able to customize your e-book. The exterior will be personalized with your own color and texture preference. You will be able to change the font style and size to suit your aesthetic taste and eyesight.

Books Made-to-Order

Textbooks rarely correspond to the course structure that individual teachers use, and they can go out of date almost as soon as they hit the shelves. Photocopying has already cut a huge chunk out of the textbook market because it gives end users the option of structuring their own learning materials by assembling bits of existing books and periodicals.

The new media operating in a Bagel-friendly environment is taking this trend to its logical conclusion and allowing learners to compile their own custom textbooks and course-kits on demand. Users can select sections, chapters, illustrations, or paragraphs from a variety of texts and assemble them into a cohesive collection (from the user's perspective) which may be printed out in an edition of one. This is already taking place on many campuses in North America.

To Have and to Hold

There will always be items that we cherish because of the way they look and feel, and books are no exception. Coffee-table books, which include the general category of art books, are an example. Some printed materials beg to be touched, some pages yearn to be gently turned, and some printed books are meant be opened for shared viewing. These will survive and thrive because they are designed to optimize a book's form factors.

OnLine Books

Because books do not lend themselves to be read on-line they have not made a rapid transition to networked delivery. The marketing and sale of physical books, however, has already moved to the Internet. In 1998, about 20% of all the books purchased in North America will be over the Internet and this percentage will increase as more people go online and discover they can access a wider variety of titles, search them easily, and then sample a bit of their content.

E-News and E-Zines

Newspapers and magazines exhibit greater interactivity than books because they are designed to be browsed (the Web has appropriated the word browser to describe its own interactive nature). In addition, they are a more "disposable" product than books, meant to be read and then discarded. That's the reason they are making the transition to e-news and e-zines more successfully than books.

They are already chunked into bite-sized (and byte-sized) portions for quick assimilation according to a reader's tastes, needs, and time availability. They are already created and edited in digital formats before they are printed. The e-news of the future may take the electronic text as it exists on newsroom servers and make it available to readers without converting it to print. This would be simpler and much cheaper. Readers of e-news and e-zines will have filters to allow them to automatically get the news that interests them most. In addition to having control over the content categories, "I want sports and no comics please,"readers will be able to get multimedia versions of their news — audio, video, animated graphics, and so on — when they click on a static image within an e-news page.

Electronic versions of newspapers such as the *New York Times* already exist on the Internet and are very popular. Like the e-book, there will eventually be an e-news appliance similar in form to a newspaper. Content will be updated constantly by news services and available instantly to users for wireless downloading.

Some print magazines, like their coffee-table book counterparts, will survive without shifting to online delivery because their art direction and high-resolution glossy pictures are the primary attraction for their readers, not likely to be soon duplicated by other technologies. In some cases, the ads in magazines like *Vogue* are a primary attraction for readers, and will help printed magazines to thrive.

Read an E-Journal, Save a Tree

Printed journals will not survive because they are meant to be searched. Their material is indexed over many issues and a broad range of interests. Journals are particularly well suited for organization into digital databases that may be searched by author, topic, article name, key words, date of publication, and so on. That's why so many have become available on digital networks. In fact, many periodicals are being made available only in electronic formats because their readership is small and the cost of printing much higher than the cost of mounting the material on a CD-ROM or Web site.

Whereas printed journals contribute to the destruction of forests, e-journals do not, and many readers of this material appreciate the ecological benefits of the electronic delivery system. The bottom line is that journals will thrive on digital networks because that's where users can most easily and most quickly access the articles in them, when and where they need the information.

Direct Mail, Posters, Flyers

Direct mail advertisers will continue to use high-definition color printing to stimulate impulse buying, but the trend towards narrowcast demographics and personally targeted ads will shift much of their action to digital networks. When an individual logs on his or her favorite Web site, a custom-tailored advertisement will appear.

Similarly, posters, banners, and flyers with high-definition images will continue to be popular and effective forms of advertising, though pricey. Increasingly, however, these will proliferate on digital networks because it's so much less expensive to produce and distribute them there. The challenge for marketers in cyberspace will be getting past the junk mail filters.

Catalogs

Catalogs are perfect candidates for the move from print to interactive media. In the new media, users will be able to alter the colors and fabrics of items like furniture or drapes, "try on" clothing superimposed on their body images, and walk around items to get 3-D views. E-catalogs will automatically subtract items that are out of stock to avoid disappointment in ordering, and hyperlink customers to similar items that might be of interest. The addition of sound and video will bring enormous benefit to selling everything from recordings to vacation packages.

BAGEL BITS

The World Wide Web uses html — HyperText Markup Language — technology that moves control of the typeface, type size, and exact placement of images from the publisher to the user. Html accommodates users who log on to the Web with different computer systems, each with different typeface capabilities, screen resolutions, and color capabilities. This frees text from the constraints of physical type and allows users to control the display of words in a document.

This is in keeping with the Bagel Effect, but it sometimes makes for badly displayed images on some systems. The great advantage of html is that it is device-agnositic. A Web page may be viewed in full color and high-resolution on one user's monitor, while also being available on a palm-sized monochrome display in a personal organizer.

E-mail — the New Literacy

The advent of e-mail has brought a return to natural speech patterns. Because the communication is virtually immediate and because we needn't take the time and effort to address and stamp our mail, we tend to write many more e-mail messages than traditional letters, and we write them much more quickly. We use less formality, less punctuation, less capitalization, more sentence fragments, more run-on sentences, more stream-of-consciousness, and less proofing and spell-checking. In fact, e-mail is closer in form to the syntax and flow of normal speech.

This new literacy, e-literacy, is of great concern to some while others find it liberating. Many editors, experts who help organize and proof copy, react to this chapter as if I were putting a dagger in their hearts. Kids, on the other hand, take to e-mail instantly. When he was five, my grandson was able to send me a very comprehensible e-mail, although he had not yet learned to write with a pencil.

E-mail and the Web have greatly increased literacy. Kids on the Net are reading much more than their parents did when they were young. The text is not as manicured and well articulated as it was in the books of yesteryear, but there's lots of it, and kids can't navigate to what they're looking for without reading and typing words. Some would argue that e-literacy is not equivalent to print literacy and they would be correct. There is no good argument, however, that print literacy is somehow superior to e-literacy. The measurement should be the quality of communication, not its form of expression.

E-literacy reinforces the Bagel Effect because it moves control from teachers, schools, and publishers to writers and readers who gain freedom over the input and output of their thoughts.

Repurposing Legacy Content

It's interesting that legacy print content — books, magazines, and journals — is being rapidly absorbed into the first wave of new media by converting the content to digital formats and republishing it on interactive networks and CD-ROMs. This is known as "repurposing" content, and it is very attractive to publishers because the largest cost factor, the original planning and creation of the content, has already been absorbed into the business model of its first use. Repurposing has obvious attractions for the print industry because it allows the transfer of equity from existing content to the new business models.

Repurposing content is not a new concept. The film industry has been very successful in repurposing their films for television and then for video stores. Radio did it with their dramas and quiz shows when TV was introduced. Interestingly enough, the technology of printing itself parlayed the legacy content of monastic scribal works into valuable mass-market products for the new industry.

Amazing Amazon

Three years after making its first online sale, the *amazon.com* Web site has become the third-largest bookseller in North America. Jeff Bezos, a summa com laude Princeton graduate, who started the Web site in 1994, became a billionaire in 1998 when his 20 million shares traded for $105 (US). The irony is that books, the most successful e-commerce product to date, were supposed to be endangered by the Internet. Jeff points out in interviews that his aim was to transport online book-selling back to the days of the small bookseller, who got to know each customer's reading habits and would recommend titles he or she might enjoy. In that sense, he is very much in tune with the Bagel Effect, more so than the large book chains like Barnes & Noble, whose bookstore business is being cannibalized by the Amazon Web site. Another noticeable Bagel Effect: as customers become empowered with increased choice, they are expanding their purchases from mass-marketed bestsellers to poetry, academic tomes, and forgotten treasures of years gone by.

BAGEL BITS

Print technology was instrumental in creating the divergent and specialized information glut that surrounds us. From this perspective, Gutenberg was an information villain. His good intention was to democratize access to information but one result is a society suffering from information overload.

The future of print lies in the ability of publishers to embrace the new media and find ways to bridge the old and new using their common denominator of text. This book is being published in print, but it was written in an outline processor so that the topic headings that appear throughout the chapters may be used as a natural mark-up for searching the text in electronic forms. In this way, an increasing number of text materials will be chunked appropriately for delivery on existing and new media.

13 RECORDS
Music Is an Experience, Not a CD

When Thomas Edison patented the phonograph, its primary commercial use was expected to be a dictating machine for business. The technology survived almost unchanged for nearly a century, but its commercial use quickly moved to entertainment. Today, about $50 billion worth of music recordings are sold annually throughout the world.

Of all the twentieth-century media, music was the first to go digital. SONY and Phillips, two of the world's consumer electronics titans, joined forces to make the compact disc a standard. CDs made vinyl LPs obsolete. This change of media required that music lovers buy new digital players for their homes, offices, cottages, and automobiles.

The digital medium brought superior sound quality and clarity. Turntable rumble, wow, flutter, and record hiss, which had degraded LP sound, were gone forever. The success of music CDs was so great that within a decade they had completely replaced vinyl LPs and 45-rpm singles. Record companies converted their legacy catalogs of recordings into the new digital standard so they could be reissued in the CD format. Consequently, the music industry has a huge store of content that is ready for distribution on the new media.

Mass Production, Mass Market

Like printing, the record business evolved in a mass-production and mass-marketing mode. Record companies have been at the center of this system, manufacturing and distributing only those music titles whose sales expectations are high enough to warrant the cost of physical production, warehousing, transportation, insurance, piracy, and marketing. The individual musical taste of the consumer has been submerged under the commercial realities of the business.

As in printing, the duplication of recordings is only profitable when you manufacture many copies of a single title, and as in printing, this technology will soon be waning as consumers assert their new power to control the choice of content they consume.

Let's Play

The original CDs, like their predecessors, were a play-only technology. The key to mass production has been the record pressing plant which stamps out inexpensive copies of records in machines that are the equivalent of printing presses. All consumers get the same liner notes, the same packaging, and the same assembly of songs on a CD. Until recently, the consumer has not had the ability to change the material on a disc.

Consumers Program Tracks

Although LPs and CDs are both play-only media, CDs brought a significant advance in addition to their better quality — they allow the user to play individual songs on a disc *and* to program the order that songs are played in. This additional control given to the user has been very popular and has led to new players that allow you to insert several CDs at the same time and then program songs from among the different CDs. These two features begin to approximate the random access technology available for content residing on computer disks. The popularity of these features was a clear confirmation that users wish to control the compilation and scheduling of music they listen to.

A second technology that came to the fore in the second half of this century is tape recording. Unlike plastic discs, metallic tape may be recorded in affordable appliances available to the public. By the 1960s, audiocassettes had taken hold as the predominant standard for recordable tape. Although the sound quality is inferior to discs, cassettes thrive because of two attributes:

- They can be played in moving vehicles while LPs can not;

- They allow consumers to assemble their own song compilations by recording individual selections from CDs, and off the radio.

DATs the Problem

In the 1990s, digital audiocassettes — DATs — became available, and they have the same convenience as analog cassettes while overcoming the problem of poor quality. From an industrial perspective, the DAT standard posed a significant threat. They moved power to consumers by allowing them to control the choice of content (as with cassettes), plus they sounded as good as CDs. The threat was simple: in a creampuff industry skewed towards centrally controlled and mass-produced products, DATs allowed choice and selection to move to the edges of the system, to consumers.

The industry quickly plugged the leak in their boat. They pressured the DAT recorder manufacturers to install copy-prohibition devices in their machines that prevent users from doing what the medium was *designed* to do — make copies of digital music. As a result, this excellent technology has been relegated to professional applications where the recorders are used for new musical content, not copying CDs. In addition, the digital technology has converged with the computer industry where DATs are used as backup systems for digital computer data.

Now that we are in Bagel Effect times, the power balance between consumers and mass producers is changing radically and we will soon see a major shift in the way recordable technologies are used by music lovers.

Record Your Own CD

By the late 1990s, the price of computer hard disks dropped low enough that they could be used to store digital song files downloaded from the Internet. The Internet quickly evolved as a repository of music files that could be downloaded by netizens and assembled on their computers to form a custom song library. The problems remain that full-fidelity stereo music consumes very large (and expensive) amounts of disk space and takes a long time to download over a network with a modem connection.

To ameliorate these problems, Web sites compress the music so that it takes up less space on the serving disk, takes less time to download, and takes up less space on the user's computer disk. In the compression process, however, quality is lost, and so this technique has not been a satisfactory substitute for buying CDs. Nonetheless, many record industry people see downloading of individual songs as a viable business in the future. At least one Web site, Music Boulevard, currently allows users to download songs at a dollar each and pays record companies, music publishers, and other stakeholders their share of royalties as if the songs had been sold on a physical CD in a retail store. But even with hard disk prices low, the cost of storing data on a recordable medium will always be higher than the cost of mass producing a CD, and so it remains to be seen whether consumers will be willing to pay a premium for this type of use.

Try-and-Buy

An interim approach to using the new media for music is to audition a track from a CD over the Internet at a lower quality, and then, if you like the music, order it directly from the site operator. This so-called try-and-buy retailing is becoming very popular and has begun to seriously cannibalize record sales from traditional retail stores. By 1998, about 15% of all CD sales were made through the Internet.

Music-on-Demand

The Holy Grail for consumers is music-on-demand. Using a technology called "streaming," any music title can be sent to a user in real-time, without downloading the file to the computer. Think of it as a new form of radio over the Internet in which users have access to all the music on CDs. They can search for selections easily and then have the music played in their home over the digital network. The main obstacle to this application has been the Internet itself, which has not had the technical capacity to deliver full-fidelity digital music in real-time. Those days are nearing an end, however.

Today there are many networks that can deliver full-fidelity music. Shaw and Rogers Cable market their cable-modem @Home.Canada service and many telephone companies have deployed their broadband services. Both of these can deliver music-on-demand today at very attractive prices. The stumbling block has been the business model. How will stakeholders be paid for ephemeral (instant and temporary) listening when they can no longer charge for a physical CD product? The *Globe and Mail* summed it up in an article on March 28, 1998: "The majors totally understand the appeal from the customer's perspective, but they want to make sure this doesn't cannibalize sales."

A New Music Business

Consider the following example of a new business model that could substitute online listening to music for the physical CDs.

Music is delivered ephemerally when it is performed on the radio, in taverns, in shopping malls, on airplanes, at concerts, and so on. The music composer and publisher are paid for its use by a performing rights society. In Canada, that's SOCAN — the Society of Composers, Authors, and Music Publishers of Canada. SOCAN has agreements with similar societies throughout the world by which it represents foreign music in Canada. These foreign societies similarly represent Canadian music in their countries so that each society can deliver a performing license for virtually all the world's music in their own country. In Canada, SOCAN collects about $25 million annually from radio stations for a blanket license to broadcast any music they wish.

The record business is not based on ephemeral music. Consumers get to keep the physical CDs and play them as many times as they want. This business in Canada accounts for about $1 billion in annual retail sales representing fifty million CDs sold in retail stores for about $20 each.

A record company, after paying for the cost of manufacturing, packaging, and distributing the disc, ends up with about $6.00 for each disc sold. From this $6.00 the record company pays songwriters, music publishers, performing artists, and producers about $2.25, leaving it with $3.75 to advertise and promote its products, run their business, and, with any luck, make a profit.

If music were delivered on digital networks instead of by radio and compact disc, the stakeholders would expect to get paid at least as much money as they now get. Otherwise, there would be no incentive to move to the new distribution channel.

The following table and graph compare the potential costs of music to consumers with and without delivering the physical CD. It assumes that record companies, composers, publishers, artists, and producers would earn the same money they do now.

	Music Only	Music+CD
Record Company	$3.75	$3.75
Writer/Publisher	$1.00	$1.00
Artist/Producer	$1.25	$1.25
Distributor	$2.00	$4.00
CD + Packaging	$0.00	$2.00
Record Store	$0.00	$8.00
Cost To Customer	$8.00	$20.00

Figure 13.1 — Music Without CDs

Savings are achieved as a result of eliminating the cost of manufacturing the physical CD, packaging it, and selling it in a retail store. When the musical works are accessed through digital networks, the distribution costs are lower because there is no warehousing, transportation, insurance, and so on. Let's assume these overhead costs would be reduced to $2 instead of the $4 in the case of physical CDs. This means that the cost to a consumer could come down to $8 from the $20 now charged at retail stores.

In order to pay all the stakeholders as much income as they now receive, a new digital distribution system would need to generate $425 million annually.

$400 million = 50 million CDs x $8 each to the consumer

+

$ 25 million for lost radio revenue (assume radio dies)

$425 million

Figure 13.2 — New Music Business

About 17 million Canadians (teens and adults under 50 years old) currently purchase on average three CDs a year (that results in the 50 million units sold) at a cost of $60 (3 x $20). If you could offer the same customers access to *all* recorded music instead of just the three CDs they purchased this year (plus the balance in their collection), they would be better off financially and better served musically. This $60-a-year per customer would generate more than twice the current income to music stakeholders — $1.02 billion. The same music service could in fact be delivered digitally for only $25 annually and still generate the current $425 million to music stakeholders.

Although this pricing example may not be the one ultimately adopted by the music industry, it illustrates how digital content-on-demand can be a win-win situation for both content owners — the artists and music companies — and consumers. It will doubtless replace the existing music business eventually. From the perspective of the Bagel Effect, it is the only business model in tune with the times.

List-Based Music

Once music is available on-demand there are many ways it could be accessed. One of these is by a list. You could make a list of all the songs you like best and voilà! You have programmed your own personal radio station. You could make a list of music you'd like to play for friends when they visit for dinner on Saturday evening, music your kids like to listen to when they come home from school, and so on.

Such a system has been in operation for Stonehaven West, a southern Ontario community, since 1997. Although they started out with only two thousand music selections (by the turn of the century such systems could have millions of selections available), they love the service. It is primo Bagel — users have maximum freedom and control.

The Big Guys

Today, only a few multinational companies control the distribution of music throughout the world. There is an enormous barrier for other companies trying to enter the business because of the infrastructure cost of warehousing, trucking, manufacturing, national advertising, and so on. In the next few decades this will change as the infrastructure cost of digital networks is borne by millions of companies in thousands of market niches.

The oft-quoted future in which creators (in this case composers, musicians, and recording artists) make their works available around the world without dealing with the "tyranny" of publishers, radio stations, and record companies is here today on the Internet. There are already examples of bands that cannot today get a record deal and cannot get airplay, but are nonetheless selling their music on the Net.

It would be naive, however, to predict that this method of self-distribution will be the norm. While it will enormously broaden the choice of titles for consumers and the opportunities for artists, most consumers will continue to be driven by products that have mass advertising and promotion. There is no better way to drive global demand than with large companies who will spend big bucks in marketing and have the expertise to make hits.

The Little Guys and Girls

Without a doubt, the biggest change enabled by digital distribution is that small independent artists can, for the first time, make their works available directly to consumers. Some of these artists have eager audiences that are too small to justify the cost of national marketing and promotion campaigns. These audiences will be able to find them on the Web and buy their products. Other artists will start out as self-produced, self-promoted, and self-distributed on the Web and, when they develop a large enough following, will be signed by the majors for large-scale marketing. Lastly, the enormous group of music hobbyists, whose aim is primarily to have fun with music, will connect with each other to exchange their work and discuss it. It is conceivable that some of this music will find its way into the commercial mainstream as well.

BAGEL BITS

The prognosis for the record industry according to the Bagel Effect is:

- more suppliers;
- more variety of content;
- more choice for consumers;
- direct sales between creators and users;
- fewer pre-packaged record albums;
- a continuing role for large record companies focused on marketing and promotion.

14 TELEVISION
TV Without Broadcasting

In the nineteen twenties when David Sarnoff (later President of RCA) presented the idea for commercial radio to his associates, they said, "The wireless music box has no imaginable commercial value. Who would pay for a message sent to nobody in particular?"

This quote is another example of insiders not recognizing an impending industrial shift. In their time, they were wrong of course, but given the cyclic nature of history, their observation becomes correct today from the perspective of the Bagel Effect with its decreased reliance on broadcasting. After all, the only reason we pay for a message sent to nobody in particular is that we haven't been able to get a message sent to someone in particular.

Broadcasting Is Linear

Broadcasting, like books, is a linear medium. A television program starts at the beginning and continues unabated until it reaches the end. Unlike conversation, television removes the participant from social interaction. Television's detractors speak of the zombie-like state that TV viewers assume, but it can be argued that this is no different than being absorbed in other media, like books. In fact, the television couch potato resembles the bookworm when he withdraws from interaction and concentrates on the story unfolding in front of him.

Although watching television is not interactive, it is somewhat more social than reading because the viewer frequently shares the appliance and the experience with others. Few people get together with their friends to sit in corners of a room and read books, but friends and family do watch television together. Also from the social perspective, commercial breaks are a welcome opportunity to socialize and discuss the program, not to mention to get a snack or make a trip to the bathroom.

Antennas

Governments carve out television channels from the available bandwidth in the electromagnetic spectrum. The number of broadcast channels is therefore limited, and each is a very valuable resource. About a dozen channels are available in any local area.

Broadcast signals have to navigate trees, hills, and tall buildings en route to the rooftop antenna, so they can be received only within a few dozen miles of the transmitter before the signal begins to degrade. This requires a broadcast system assembled from many local stations, each with limited local broadcasting reach. The local stations cannot afford to produce the high-quality program that audiences desire, so they affiliate with a national network that acquires programs and makes them available to the local station.

The centrally controlled broadcast system is thus an artifact of broadcasting on the electromagnetic spectrum through air, and of the decision to design television sets as cheaply as possible, which in the days of vacuum tubes meant a minimum of electronic processing. With the advent of digital technologies, neither of these technology-based decisions is valid today. With the advent of the Bagel Effect, the time is right to switch the entire paradigm of television to a user-centered model. As we'll see, this is exactly what's happening.

Cable TV — The Big Antenna

Cable TV started as a big antenna in an unobstructed location feeding a bunch of houses that couldn't get good reception of broadcast channels from rooftop antennas. By 1950, 70 cable systems served 14,000 subscribers nationwide.

By 1960, cable operators could pick up broadcast signals from hundreds of miles away. Access to these "distant signals" changed the focus of cable's role from transmitting local broadcast signals to providing new programming choices.

By the 1980s, the antenna that used to get its signal from ground stations had evolved into a system of huge antennas that received signals from satellites in space, amplified them, and retransmitted them to homes on new channels.

Today, cable television is available to approximately 97% of television households in the United States, with more than 70 million North American households now subscribing to cable services.

The bandwidth available for television signals in a coaxial cable is greater than in air, because there are no competing signals from cellphones, wireless microphones, walkie-talkies, radio stations, or other electromagnetic devices. This allows cablecos to squeeze many more channels into their consumer services than you can get from on-air local broadcasters. The average subscriber receives more than 80 channels of programming.

From 1984 through 1992, the cable television industry spent about $20 billion wiring North America, and billions more on program development, the largest private construction project since World War II.

Because the cost of installing the infrastructure is so high, regulators have given cable companies regional monopolies, like the telephone companies. Like other areas of deregulation, the cable TV industry is about to change, as telecommunications companies begin to enter this previously restricted market.

Satellite TV

There are many rural, agricultural, and remote areas in Canada and the United States where the cost of installing coaxial cables is too high for a local cableco to run a profitable business from the small population of users. These areas have taken advantage of satellite delivery systems that deliver signals to residential satellite antennas using the same technologies they use for beaming signals to cablecos.

The advantage of satellite television is that reception is excellent because the signal does not have to travel through long coaxial cables that degrade the image. The disadvantage has been the cost of the antenna and decoding electronics. The price has now become competitive and satellite television is beginning to erode the cable TV market, even in urban areas.

ITV — Interactive Television

Interactive Television — ITV — requires a special set-top box that allows each user to customize the television program. ITV shifts the emphasis from the broadcaster to the viewer who can control additional sub-channels of pictures and text by sending messages back to the cable television operator. Initial offerings have been very simple, offering such features as overlaying sports statistics during a game.

ITV services such as Videotron's UBI in Quebec have been deployed using proprietary non-standard systems and set-top boxes. Set-top boxes are next-generation cable converters with computer components that allow them to perform additional functions such as video overlays and picture-in-a-picture.

ITV is a last-gasp attempt by the television industry to include interactivity in its programming in order to satisfy viewers seeking control over their programs. Only a few years ago, ITV was touted as the hottest thing since sliced bread, the broadcasters' version of the Infoway. It has stalled, however, and major telcos, cablecos, and Hollywood multinationals have lost billions by betting on it.

Web TV

Many people believe that the television set will triumph as the appliance of choice for Infoway consumers. One argument is that there is a greater penetration in North America of television sets (several per household) than computers (less than half of households have them). The second argument is that television sets cost less than computers do.

Since ITV has been a flop, the television industry has turned to bringing computer technologies and the World Wide Web to your television sets. This is accomplished by using a next-generation set-top box that is essentially a computer dressed in channel-changer attire. The set-top box has a Web browser built in and puts an image of the Web page on your TV screen.

This Web TV is a huge improvement over ITV because it builds on the tremendous value of the Internet and World Wide Web. The Web page can cover the entire screen, or appear as a window within a normal television screen. Alternatively, you can have a window of normal TV within the Web page image.

Although major companies like SONY and Microsoft have injected very big bucks into Web TV, there are still questions that need to be resolved if it is to become a consumer hit, questions that have as much to do with socialization as technology. Since you watch TV from a distance, it's not easy to read the small text that fills most Web pages. When Web TV emulates ITV, this problem can be overcome by designing Web pages with large-sized text using fonts that display well on TVs.

1999 should bring a major roll-out of Web TV appliances, as broadband providers roll out Web applications tailored for these new devices. They will feature shopping channels that display merchandise in different colors and sizes, and interactive TV guides that will preset your TV to switch channels at appropriate times for your favorite programs.

A larger problem for Web TV proponents is that television is a one-way medium; sets only receive signals. Until the cable television infrastructure is rebuilt to accept two-way traffic, Web TV must rely on standard telephone lines to get the signal back to the Internet, which is an additional cost for the viewer. Even when there's a return path, you still need a keyboard of some sort if you wish to access Web sites, since many of them require you to type in data in addition to navigating around the screen.

ATV

In December 1996, the Federal Communications Commission (FCC) mandated the biggest change to television since the introduction of color, when it legislated a new digital television standard. This was a compromise worked out by the broadcast, computer, and consumer electronics industries. The new television system is called advanced television — ATV.

Canada is following suit. ATV broadcasting in the major centers is slated to begin in 1999, and elsewhere in Canada by 2004. The existing analog television system would then cease operating in Canada by 2007. The Canadian Cable Television Association reckons it will cost about $1 billion to make available just thirty channels of wide-screen high-definition digital television. That's just the cost of changing the delivery systems. The digital broadcast systems will add another half billion to that cost.

This standard for the next generation of television sets pits powerful consumer electronics firms against innovative PC titans because the next generation of PCs and TVs will speak the same language — digital. Virtually all the broadcast equipment now used, from cameras to special effects units, will be phased out. All the production and technical people working in the industry will have to be retrained on the new digital equipment.

This transition will be a bonanza for equipment manufacturers like SONY and Panasonic, who will sell new equipment to every consumer, television station, and production facility. However, hundreds of thousands of people now working in the television industry are at risk. They will lose their jobs unless they upgrade their skills.

The FCC gave broadcasters about $70 billion worth of free, new digital broadcast channels (one for each analog channel they now operate) in return for a promise that by 2006 all the current analog TV channels will go off the air. That means that in 2006 none of the existing television sets will work with the new television content. This aggressive timetable for changing the technical television standard will drive all segments of the television industry at the start of the twenty-first century. The first ATV broadcasts are scheduled to begin in 1998.

The advent of digital ATV will allow manufacturers to build in the electronics that now reside in set-top and Web TV boxes. The cost of this will be a fraction of the set-top or Web TV boxes. The result will be one of the first consumer electronic devices worthy of the title "Infoway appliance." So the winner of the "Is it the TV or computer?" contest is no one, since it will be the new converged ATVs that will likely spark the mass acceptance of the Infoway.

These new television sets will be the computer monitors of tomorrow, lowering the cost of entry for new computer buyers because of the economies of scale for manufacturers who will use the same technologies for both TV and computers. Digital TVs will contain an increasing number of microprocessors to incorporate functions ranging from today's channel-changing boxes, to Internet gateways, to interactivity. In reality, they will become monitors with built-in computers.

HDTV

HDTV stands for High Definition Television. HDTV was first introduced in Japan about fifteen years ago in the hopes of creating an industrial bonanza for manufacturers of consumer and professional television products. The idea was simple — a new standard would force all suppliers and users to buy new equipment. SONY spearheaded the effort that was based on adding more resolution to the existing television system. The quality of the picture was outstanding, but this first HDTV introduction failed nonetheless.

The effort failed for two key reasons. Firstly, consumers had not been asking for higher-resolution television pictures. Focus groups showed that users perceived a greater increase in value when the sound was improved than when the number of picture elements was increased. This makes sense in light of the boom in home theaters that has been driven primarily by surround-sound. Secondly, the Japanese system was not digital; it could not work with computers.

The Americans refused to endorse the system. Their excuse was that the initial HDTV wasn't digital, a reasonable criticism. The underlying reason was that the initial HDTV standard gave Japanese companies a head start in the business. They were pre-eminent in the television business, while the Americans held sway in the computer business and saw the new TV standard as an opportunity to enter that business so long as it was based on digital computer technology.

When the Americans designed their digital HDTV system they made it interoperable with computers. They incorporated the new HDTV standards into ATV, so that new television sets would be able to receive either normal resolution or

HDTV signals. One of the advantages of the new HDTV system is that the screen resolution and aspect ratio (the squareness or elongation of the screen) are not fixed as they are for standard TVs. This is very Bagel-friendly because it allows viewers to adjust the shape and picture quality of the programs they receive.

HDTV takes up much greater bandwidth than normal television because it has about four times the resolution, about the same quality as 16 mm film. Therefore, it requires four channels of normal television to transmit the signal. Fortunately, digital signals can be compressed considerably, so the number of channels may stay the same or even increase depending on the picture resolution and quality (amount of compression) that broadcasters decide on for each channel.

Five Hundred Channels

A broadcaster can fit many new digital channels in the space of one old television channel. The multiplication factor is currently about five to one. That is, if we can receive one hundred analog channels now, we will be able to receive five hundred digital channels. Of course, if broadcasters send all the new signals in HDTV format, we're back to just over a hundred channels, since HDTV takes up four times the bandwidth.

Most likely, broadcasters will transmit programs at different resolutions according to the requirements of the programs and the tolerance of their audiences. Movies would likely be broadcast in HDTV because the original films have very high resolution and contain a wealth of information in the pictures. Normal resolution might be sufficient for a newscast or a game show.

Some of the channel bandwidth may not be used for television programs at all, since a broadcaster can use a portion of the digital bandwidth for any converged digital source — wireless paging, Internet provision, or background music to name a few. These features take up a much smaller band-width than television and so many more services will be available in a much greater variety than the current televi-sion-only channels.

No one is predicting that advertising revenue will also increase by a factor of five. The existing funds for producing television programs will be split into many more productions whose budgets will, on average, be smaller. This has already happened with the new cable channels that were introduced in the early '90s. Their programming is on average much lower in cost than that on national networks.

TV and Eyeballs

During the twentieth century, the concepts of mass media, mass audience, and mass advertising reached its peak. These concepts dovetailed with the advent of broadcast television, which, at heart, is a system that delivers mass audiences to national advertisers. The vernacular speaks of delivering eye-balls to advertisers at a cost of so many dollars-per-thousand.

This advertising model breaks down as we move to hundreds of cable channels, each catering to a narrow interest. In this world the value of a thousand eyeballs for one show can't be compared to the value of a thousand eyeballs for another because the quality and loyalty of the audience vary greatly in narrow markets. A fishing program may not attract a huge audience but almost everyone who watches it will buy a piece of fishing gear when the season hits and a van or sport utility vehicle within a few years.

As programs move to define themselves not by mass markets but by narrow interest groups such as home improvement or science fiction, the TV model approaches the audience-focused Internet and ITV models favored by the Bagel Effect. The Internet has already cannibalized $1 billion in annual advertising revenue from television, and it's still in its infancy.

Broadcasting Will Wither

As users take control of their entertainment and information, broadcasting will wither. A broadcaster by definition selects programs and schedules them. But Internet-type TV services are cannibalizing regular TV, with viewers increasingly controlling selection and scheduling — what they want to watch and when they want to watch it. In the long term, broadcasting as we know it will be greatly reduced, focusing on programs and events that must be viewed as they occur live for maximum value. Already, the once-powerful TV networks ABC, NBC, and CBS have seen their nightly audience drop from 60% in 1993 to 38% in 1998. The most loyal broadcast TV viewers are over fifty years old, a diminishing demographic.

Broadcasting may wind up as just one of a number of parallel services, a button alongside Programs-on-demand, perhaps. It may be more likely that in the future we will have just a few channels: Channel 1 might be LIVE, Channel 2 could be MOVIES, Channel 3 GAMES, and so on. Within these channels, viewers would choose specific programs from hundreds of suppliers.

Program Categories

Let's examine some television program categories and see how they may fare in the wake of the Bagel Effect. Some programs will stay on the equivalent of network television channels, and others will migrate to on-demand services. Many programs will have one life on network television and another one on on-demand services. This is similar to the market today for syndication, except programs only go into syndication after they have survived several seasons of network exposure. Not so in the new television world.

If viewers are in control, some will want to see a sitcom at a fixed day and time every week and others may want to watch several episodes every second weekend. Even those who want a fixed schedule may want differing fixed days and differing fixed times. Almost all viewers will want the flexibility of catching up on a missed episode, even if a series is on a network.

News

News will continue to be one of the cornerstones of the television schedule. News needs to be up-to-the-minute and live. It is one of the areas where networks excel. Local news will become available not only where it was produced, but anywhere. A Montrealer vacationing in Florida will be able to watch the local Montreal newscast there.

Sports

Like the news, sports is a program category that is most valuable when it's live. How exciting is it to watch a hockey game when the final scores have already been posted in the news? Some sports programs may well have significant value after the events have passed. Basketball fanatics might well want to watch several of the Saturday games that were on at the same time. With on-demand programs, you could watch one game live and then schedule the others when it suits you.

Concerts

Concerts fall into two categories that dictate how they will be delivered. Live events have high value because of their timeliness, and are suitable for television networks. Consider the Live Aid concert a few years back, for example. Viewers throughout the world tuned in on the same day and the event was covered by the news media. The impact was much greater than if the concert were just made available as an on-demand program. Most other concerts will be on-demand services, allowing you to watch them when you have the time and inclination.

Films

Feature films don't belong on regular television. Here's why:

- Their length argues for a pause button (for snack and pee breaks);

- They have to be cropped to fit the television format;
- They were designed for high information density exhibition in cinemas.

They fit perfectly in the new home-theater set-ups. Home-theater equipment is the fastest growing segment of the consumer electronics business. The equipment includes a large screen television set and multi-channel hi-fi gear to process the Dolby surround-sound and other simulated theater acoustics. A VHS videotape player is adequate for playback but these systems really shine when you use one of the new DVD players. Sound is awesome and the picture is great on a big screen.

With this sort of quality available from your local video store, why would you watch movies on regular television? The answer is that, likely, you won't. Movies on television can be a huge program category, but only when viewers get them on-demand, and with as great a choice as they have at the local video store.

Game Shows

Game shows are not time-sensitive. I have friends who get together for *Jeopardy* parties and watch four or more episodes, one after the other. On the other hand, some people like to know that when they come home from work on Thursday, *Jeopardy* will be on the tube. They will be accommodated in both cases by the new on-demand services. Because game shows are relatively inexpensive to produce, they may well proliferate outside the boundaries of regular television. They may migrate to the Internet where users can get a more interactive as well as a more convenient experience.

Soaps

People who watch soaps really get into them. The stories are sequential, so if you miss an episode or two you can lose the plot line. Usually aficionados have at least one friend that also watches the same programs and they discuss the machinations and transformations of the characters frequently. This gives soaps a timeliness that approaches the news and sports. They may well survive on the new television.

Like sports, however, if you can't watch an episode when it's normally scheduled, you will want to have the opportunity to catch up on it later. Viewers will want these on-demand as well.

Sitcoms

Sitcoms are different than soaps because the episodes are not generally sequential. It doesn't matter much if you miss one. Keeping that in mind, the Bagel Effect would suggest that these will migrate to on-demand services, although they may continue on normally scheduled television, albeit with a much reduced audience.

Music

MUCH Music, MTV, and other services should survive on television as background music services, much as radio functions today. People who are interested in paying attention to the videos will want to take the effort of programming their own choices from an on-demand service.

Other Programs

Documentaries, nature, and history are some program categories that are not time-sensitive. Training or entertainment programs such as fishing, cooking, crafts, and home improvement shows are perfect candidates for on-demand services.

Transition Stations — Citytv

If we use history as a guide, few companies that now dominate the broadcast TV world will be capable of making the transition to the new frameworks for success. Nonetheless, there are always some companies able to grasp the new opportunities.

Toronto's Citytv has been at the forefront of bringing interactivity under its corporate umbrella. Under the direction of television guru Moses Znaimer, the CHUM Group, Citytv's parent company, is building an international reputation for combining traditional broadcasting with new interactivity. For many years, it has offered fax-in, phone-in, and e-mail interactivity to its TV audiences, not to mention it's *Speaker's Corner* video booths. Citytv was the first Canadian station to start its own web service — *City Interactive.*

City Interactive is an entertainment web service with a lean, audience-focused, and Bagel-friendly approach to the future. With a small budget and a dedicated staff, they have levered the equity of their broadcast siblings — Citytv, MUCH Music, Music Pulse, and Bravo! — into a popular America On-line site, and several Internet sites.

Citytv's close contact with their audience bodes well for their future. As audiences continue to identify less with broadcasters than with individual programs, broadcasters need to establish clear identities if they are to survive the transition to consumer choice.

BAGEL BITS

As interactive television merges with computers on broadband networks, the need for large volumes of high-quality interactive programs will skyrocket. Professionals from both realms will merge into a new production industry to meet the demand. Don't send your kid to law school. Encourage her to study content creation — music, film, drama, literature, and the like. There will be lots of work in these fields. Be wary of media arts courses that teach traditional television and film skills; they will soon be obsolete.

15 CINEMA
Movies Without Film

"Who the hell wants to hear actors talk?"

— Harry Warner, Warner Brothers, 1927.

Fortunately for Harry Warner, the audience reaction to sound with movies was so immediate and positive that the entire industry adopted the new technology almost overnight, including Warner Brothers. If only some film studios had moved to talkies, the ones that didn't would today be minor footnotes to film historians. It's relevant to examine whether the new digital technologies available to Hollywood filmmakers will have the same impact on the business that sound did.

Movies, like computer games, are all-engrossing. The extended view on the wide screen in a cinema occupies most of our vision. The information density (picture and sound resolution multiplied by the frame rate) is very high, so watching a movie doesn't allow the viewer's imagination to participate as much as with books or television. In short, you go to the movies with the attitude:"Do it to me."

Movies do not lend themselves to user control. Experiments in interactive cinema in which the audience gets to choose story paths have not been successful because people go to the movies to suspend their disbelief, not to contribute to the dramatic line. Some of the best writers in the world hone their art and craft in order to create these cultural mythologies and commentaries. In the medium of cinema, the producer will continue to control the product.

Many of the Bagel Effects that have influenced television do not apply well to cinema. While television has captured the audience's attention for real-life and localized stories, cinema has increasingly focused on expensive blockbuster movies with big-name stars, lots of action and special effects, and stories with international appeal, all far removed from everyday life. These projects naturally gravitate to the large multinational entertainment conglomerates — the majors — and are at the opposite end of the spectrum from Bagel Effect productions.

A predictable Bagel Effect is that content and services move out to end users rather than vice versa. But the advantages of moving cinema content to your home are cancelled if you want to get away from your kids or go out for a date on the town.

Nonetheless, the film production and distribution industries will change radically because of Bagel Effects. On the production side digitization will bring creators much closer to audiences, and on the distribution side the mass production of film prints will give way to movies-almost-on-demand delivered digitally to theaters.

Digital Effects

Paramount Picture's 1994 feature film *Forrest Gump* marked a turning point in modern filmmaking. Until that film, most Hollywood special effects were done using film labs, models, stop-action single frame photography, and matte paintings — realistic backgrounds filmed with actors and props in front of them. Even the *Star Wars* movies used mostly mechanical contrivances and multi-exposure film techniques for their special effects. Although computer-based digital effects were used for animations, action, and fantasy sequences, they were judged too distracting for use in dramatic dialog-filled scenes.

Forrest Gump, however, moved the art and science of digital image processing to a higher level. In this movie the lead actors and foreground objects were digitally manipulated in scenes that were dramatic in nature, scenes that used ordinary characters in ordinary settings, scenes that gave audiences the greatest opportunity to detect image manipulations. One of the actors portrayed a one-legged character in the film. In real life, he is a fully functioning biped whose leg was digitally removed from every frame of the scenes he was in. In other scenes Tom Hanks, the actor who portrayed Forrest Gump, was filmed in front of a blank background and his image digitally inserted into old footage that included President Kennedy.

When Steven Spielberg shot *Jurassic Park*, he was ready to create some of the lead characters, dinosaurs, entirely on digital computers. He hedged his bet by constructing dinosaur models for some scenes and integrated them with the digitally created reptiles. But by the end of shooting in 1993, he was convinced that the computer animations were just as realistic as the models and much simpler to use.

Digital People

By the time Jim Cameron shot his 1997 Oscar award-winning *Titanic*, he had used many digital effects in his previous films. But *Titanic* was the first to use digital people. Hundreds of actors who would normally have been hired as extras and stunt persons were modeled on computers and digitally inserted into scenes. The most spectacular stunts, where passengers and crew were falling from the boat into the ocean, were created with digital people, a much safer and less expensive process than trying to do the stunts live on the set.

Virtual Actors Join the Cast

These advances have set the stage for general use of virtual actors. By the start of the next millennium, many movies will be made with a minimum of sets and actors. The leading actors will deliver their performances against blank back-drops and the balance of the imagery will be digitally composited (layered in) using digital effects. George Lucas shot the upcoming *Star Wars* movie in just this manner. It lets him concentrate on the essential performance during shooting and allows him to adjust lighting, perspectives, and other scenic elements afterwards.

In order to accomplish this magic, computer animators create three-dimensional characters based on a combination of computer-created body parts and scanned images of real people and animals. Mathematical models that simulate gravity and the internal structures of bone, muscle, and tendon then constrain the computer characters to real-life movement. Animators use procedures that describe how a character moves. A procedure-driven computer animation of a limping actor can be manipulated simply by specifying the starting configuration of his limbs, the position the character must end up in, and how fast he's moving.

As this technology becomes less expensive (and it will) these procedures will become available to people who wish to make their own films for business use or for home movies. It's reasonable to expect that you will be able to rent procedures for well-known actors and insert them in your movies. In many cases, the estates of deceased actors could license these. How about a dueling sequence with you and Douglas Fairbanks to convince your boss you can beat the competition?

This digital capability will be available within the next decade. In keeping with the Bagel Effect, these effects put more control with creators and take it away from the hundreds of technicians and actors who work on live action movies. Today you can go to Niagara Falls and have your image superimposed on a scene of the Falls. Tomorrow you'll be able to play the part of Bogart or Bacall in *Casablanca* and have it inserted into the original film footage.

What, No Film?

The biggest change in movies themselves is that they will no longer be shot on film. Film is very expensive, it's prone to scratching, and filmmaking equipment is complex and costly.

Moviemaking is a natural for conversion to digital technology. Editing has already migrated to digital technology because it is much quicker (you don't have to physically cut the film) and more versatile (you can preview effects directly in the editing unit). A digital camera would allow directors and cinematographers to preview finished scenes complete with composited backgrounds and effects, all in the camera while the principal photography is taking place.

The hurdle for digital movies is storing and manipulating the huge amount of data in a movie. Consider the following:

- A single frame of 35 mm film requires about 20 megabytes of digital storage without compression;
- A fifteen-minute sequence of movie film requires thirty of those frames every second, multiplied by sixty for each minute of film;
- This yields 18 gigabytes of information — 18 billion bytes to be stored and manipulated.

For an entire feature film, you need to shoot about twenty hours of unedited images. The storage required is so great that up until now it has not been possible to use digital cameras for high-quality motion picture photography.

However, the continuing sharp decrease in the cost of digital storage and the availability of high-resolution digital cameras are bringing digital motion picture photography into the realm of feasibility. Experiments in Hollywood today will become routine in the next few years, which will doubtless see the transition of the film industry into one which uses no film at all.

Digital Movies Last Longer

The advantages of digital storage are numerous. For one thing, digital images do not degrade over time. Film does. Film images fade, the colors shift, and every time film moves through a projector or laboratory process its quality is degraded. Distribution prints are made from second-generation negatives because after a while the printing negatives lose their quality and have to be replaced by new ones taken from the original. When you see a movie in a theater, it looks best when you're watching a new print. Prints that have been shown many times lose their crispness and show scratches onscreen.

There is great concern by film buffs that the old film masterpieces are fading away in Hollywood vaults and may never be restored to their original visual splendor. The cost of restoration is very high and the task is very delicate. There is little incentive for restoring any but the most popular and important movies. However, digital storage allows for perfect reproduction every time, whether it's the first or the two-thousandth copy.

The same technologies that can reconstruct perfect sound from a music CD with fingerprints on it can reconstruct a perfect picture from digital picture data that have been damaged in some manner. The colors never fade or change. In fact, with digital technology, it's possible to make corrections to the color balance, contrast, and brightness in each scene without degrading the image quality (just change a few numbers here and there). Color correction can be done with film as well, but a copy has to be made each time there's a change, with a corresponding loss in quality. What you will see with digital movies is exactly what the director saw in the screening room.

Print and Distribution Costs Fall

One of the largest costs associated with film technology is the cost of prints. Think of how much you pay to have a roll of film developed and printed. Those twenty-four pictures represent one second of a movie because film goes through the projector at twenty-four frames a second. In an average movie, there are about six thousand seconds of film, equivalent to six thousand rolls of film developed and printed from your camera.

When a movie is distributed, the promotional campaign is usually national because people see talk shows and the like across the country. So, to open in one thousand theaters, a distributor has to make one thousand prints. The costs are astronomical, and after the film has been through its initial peak run, these copies have lost their value. The cost is passed on to audiences.

In addition to the cost of the prints, distributors have to bear the cost of shipping the movies. Whenever you ship goods, they are subject to breakage, pilfering (that's how the bootleg copies show up in Asia), and late delivery. The films require warehousing when they're not being shown in a theater.

Digital distribution is completely different. In fact, it's essentially the same as getting data from the Internet except that the digital network needs to have a much greater capacity than the Internet.

SONY and other companies have been testing digital distribution of movies in Hollywood. The digitized movie is sent to the theater either via a landline (you can rent telephone lines from the telephone company at any capacity you need) or broadcast from a satellite like a cable TV program. The theater stores the program in a large version of the disk drives you're familiar with on your computer, and then projects the movie using a digital projector, like the ones used for trade shows.

This method of distribution eliminates the cost of making prints, shipping them, insuring them, and warehousing them. Although the cost of digital transmission and storage has been high, it is declining rapidly and will continue to do so, while the cost of film distribution is likely to remain the same.

Better Piracy Protection

One of the worst nightmares of the entertainment industry is the pirating of records and movies and their unauthorized duplication and distribution in countries that do not have strong intellectual property legislation and enforcement. These markets, like the Soviet Union and most of Asia, represent significant leakage in the global income stream.

Digital technology offers several methods of overcoming this problem and ensuring that only authorized exhibitors get the movies. Like a cable converter on your TV that descrambles television signals only when you pay your bill, decoders in authorized movie houses can be set to decode the digital movies for authorized use. Unlike the simple scrambling that is used for your analog television signals, digital codes can be changed for each use if necessary, and the movie files can be engineered to "phone home" every time a movie is shown.

Films With Global Appeal

Large-screen theaters envelop the audience in a high-information sensory experience. This lends itself to action, adventure, and scenic stories as well as stories that feature dazzling special effects, and super-realistic surround-sound. In short, theatrical movies are skewed towards high-budget extravaganzas.

In order to recoup the large investments necessary for producing these big movies ($50 million is about average nowadays), moviemakers have to focus on big-name stars and sell their movies in all the major world markets. To do so, the movies have to be translated into many languages and that discriminates against films that are culturally specific and use many local colloquialisms. That's why Woody Allen's films may win prizes at film festivals, but they don't travel well, whereas visual comedians like Jim Carrey sell well in any language, as do hunks like Sylvester Stallone and heart throbs like Brad Pitt.

The move to digital has a particularly beneficial aspect for these movies because digital technology can encompass many soundtracks within the same product. So, instead of having to make different prints for each territory, a single digital movie can be shown in many territories with the projectionist selecting the appropriate language. In fact, one of the Bagel Effect aspects of digital movies is that within a single theater, individual audience members could enjoy different language versions by using headphones. In some countries this may result in additional business for the cinemas.

Audiences Take Control

Digital cinema means more control for audiences, and that's a Bagel Effect. With films, distributors and exhibitors have to decide long in advance which films will be shown and when they will be shown because prints have to be ordered, and films have to be shipped to warehouses and then to movie theaters across the country. Digital distribution should bring the end of long line-ups at some movie theaters and empty seats at others.

One possibility will be just-in-time exhibition. You'll phone your local movie chain and book a seat for a movie you want to see. Cinema operators will be able to load-balance their multi-theater complexes so that the digital movies are projected in theaters of appropriate capacity according to audience demand. You will be guaranteed a seat and no one will have to walk along the waiting line, counting the customers to see who makes the cut.

More importantly, digital cinema will bring an entirely new business to the cinema, the back catalog. In book publishing and record sales, there are two types of business — new releases and back catalog. The back catalog in the movie business hasn't been significant because the cost of prints, distribution, and advertising are so high that it only makes business sense to show current product. The only catalog items are art films and classics that get screened occasionally at a few specialty cinemas.

In the new consumer-driven world, older films could come back at any time. Market suction could be created in many ways, such as the death of a well-known actor or the Christmas season. Until now, re-releases have been major projects, with new prints being struck, new advertising campaigns, and so on. In a few years, audiences will determine what they'll see and when.

Home Theater Gets Competitive

The greatest Bagel Effect in cinema will be an explosion of home theaters. This category of hi-fi and video equipment is already selling like hotcakes, but so far the biggest improvement has been the sound — surround-sound coming from speakers in front and back of you that simulate the full sound you'd hear in a theater.

The breakthrough, though, will be digital television that allows for much higher resolution pictures, wider images like you see in a cinema, and perfect reproduction of movies without the quality loss we now get with videotapes. Digital Video Discs (DVDs) are here today and although their quality is superb by current standards, the images they contain must still be converted back to analog formats to be displayed on normal television sets. When digital TVs begin selling in quantity, the new-format DVDs will be able to take full advantage of their capability and deliver images close to cinema quality in your own home.

The next generation of home theaters will be so high in quality that they will, for the first time, seriously cannibalize the movie-theater business. In order to get the maximum effect you'll need a good-sized room with a large front or rear-projection television. Not everyone will have the space or the money to get the full effect. But those who do will likely continue the social trend that started with today's large-screen TVs — they will invite friends over for an evening at the movies, an experience to compete with some of the smaller cinemas in multiplexes.

BAGEL BITS

By the time digital television takes hold in the early years of the twenty-first century, digital networks like the Internet will have evolved into high bandwidth distribution systems that will bring you movies-on-demand at the resolution of digital TV. Although cinemas will continue to be popular with young adults and parents wanting a night out, these home theaters will become a major entertainment activity, particularly for those who want the comforts of home along their movie experience.

So, although the impact of new technologies will not have as immediate nor as pervasive an effect on the movie industry that the addition of sound did, the changes will radically alter the business over the coming decade. With home theaters taking over the large-screen social experience of visual media, the Bagel Effect suggests that computers and their progeny will take over our individual small-screen experiences.

16 COMPUTERS
From Mainframes to PCs

"There is no reason anyone would want a computer in their home."

— Ken Olson, president, chairman and founder of Digital Equipment Corp., 1977

Here again is a historic quote from an industry leader who should have known better. Olson erred because he viewed the computer as a number-crunching device. That line of thinking worked with Digital Equipment Corp.'s (DEC'S) mainframe customers in the late '70s, but by the '90s the Bagel Effect had kicked in and DEC was no longer in business, absorbed by Compaq, one of the largest personal computer companies. DEC lost because their view of the future favored large centrally controlled systems, systems that are anathema to the Bagel Effect.

In 1997, the average family income of someone buying a Personal Computer (PC) was $50,000. In 1998, it was down to $27,000. Analysts believe the mass penetration threshold is about 60% of homes and that sales should cross that threshold by the year 2000. This will bring a critical mass of users to the Web and trigger a further explosion of computer use.

Moore's Law says that the power (speed) of computing chips doubles every eighteen months. That is, the cost of computing power is always half of what it was a year and a half ago. Gordon Moore, an Intel executive, noticed this in 1965, and it has held true for more than thirty years, so it's safe to forecast that powerful and inexpensive computers will soon be in everyone's homes. The Bagel Effect suggests that these will be networked and will bring more power, freedom, and control to end users.

Mainframes

Before desktops came on the scene, companies used mainframe computers. These are large, complex, and very reliable machines that service many users. They are costly to buy and require a dedicated team of specialists to maintain them. Mainframes rarely crash — typically once every ten years, compared to PCs' crash rate of once-a-day average.

Users access mainframes via video terminals — screens connected to the central processing unit deep within the bowels of an organization. Mainframe terminals have no local intelligence. They send keystrokes to the remote computer that does the processing and sends the results back to the terminal screen for display. A PC, on the other hand, has its own intelligence, so you can load an application locally (from a floppy disk, say) and then run it. The PC's computation is done under the control of the user.

In the early 1990s, sales of mainframe computers declined significantly. Many less powerful PCs on employees' desks were replacing the single mainframe computer that had served all the employees of a typical large company. IBM, the largest mainframe manufacturer, calculated that mainframes were more cost-effective than distributed desktop PCs, so it kept developing, building, and promoting them. When mainframe sales dropped, IBM had to reorganize its core business, and shed more than 100,000 workers.

What IBM hadn't taken into account was the Bagel Effect. The move to distributed computing had less to do with cost-saving than with power and control shifting from central management to end users. Desktop PCs took control away from central computer departments, which had imposed software, hardware, and operating system choices on employees. In Bagel Effect parlance, this was decentralization and deregulation. For employees, it was more desirable, because it allowed them to customize the look and feel, the applications, and the tools on their computer. It was a power grab, and users won.

IBM finally got the Bagel Effect message and changed its corporate structure to reflect the importance of activity at its system edges — its customers. IBM not only reorganized its product lines, but modified its corporate culture, driving sales through solutions instead of products. The company implemented a new client-oriented sales unit as a cornerstone of the new corporate organization. Instead of salespeople having responsibilities tied to specific products, they function as customer reps. They learn the customer's business, pinpoint weak areas, and provide solutions that improve the customer's profitability. That is Bagel Effect thinking — moving from supplier focus to client focus.

Desktop Computing

The shift to desktop computing may be seen as driven by Bagel Effects, not by cost. The fact that users have power and control over their desktop computers accounts for their continuing popularity, although it's a nightmare for central administrators.

PCs allow users to be in charge of their computer. They can choose the case, monitor, disk drives, memory size, input devices, utilities, and programs. They can choose the screensaver, the desk accessories, the background screen image, and customize the pull-down menus in many applications. An Internet browser lets each user pick the font style and size he or she wants, the way images are displayed, and so on.

Portable computers are one of the most significant indications of the Bagel Effect. Portables give users mobility and the greatest amount of freedom from system administrators. It's no surprise that they have become the highest growth and profit center for most computer companies. Consumers are willing to pay a premium for portables because they give them the most control over their computing environment.

The trend towards decentralized computing will accelerate as palm-sized Personal Digital Assistants gain many of the capabilities that larger portable computers have today. Portability enables users to use their appliance wherever they are, giving them the most freedom of any consumer electronic device other than cellphones. Within the next few years the difference between mobile phones and mobile computers will vanish as they become a single appliance, a consequence of Bagel Effect convergence.

LANs and HANs

WANs — Wide Area Networks — are the provenance of telcos and other infrastructure suppliers who connect cities and countries together. The little brother of a WAN is a LAN — Local Area Network. The concept of a LAN is simple. It connects computers and peripheral equipment such as printers and scanners within a home, office, building, or campus. Until a few years ago, LANs were found primarily in large businesses and institutions.

One of the important shifts in digital connectivity has been the enormous rise in popularity of LANs, and their appearance in small businesses and residences. A LAN in a home is known as a HAN — Home Area Network. We'll refer to HANs as LANs because they use the same technologies and protocols.

Ethernet, the prevalent LAN standard, combines a software protocol understood by computers and peripherals with a standard wiring specification. It was originally the domain of big businesses and governments, but you now find Ethernet networks in homes and small offices as well. The cost of connecting appliances with Ethernet has fallen to less than $100 per connected device. Many personal computers now come with Ethernet connectivity built in so all a user has to do is string an appropriate cable between computers, printers, and other networks to allow them to exchange information.

As in-home and in-office networks have become less expensive, and as the deregulated telephone industry has allowed users to control their home and office telephone wires, these have taken on new functions as the backbones of home and office LANs. It is still relatively recently that computers have connected to Web sites and other computers via modems and the Internet. Now an entire home or office can access the Wide Area Networks through LANs.

The popularity of LANs has encouraged the creation of a new class of appliance that doesn't need the storage capacity or power of a full-blown PC. The devices range from hand-held digital address books that synchronize their data with your computer, to stripped-down computers that perform many functions as well as full-featured computers.

From PC to NC

The stripped-down computer is called an NC, or Network Computer. Because the NC is always connected to a network, it can be produced without a disc drive or expansion capability. Software programs are sent to it from a network file server and data storage goes back across the network to the file server. The file server may be at home, on the Internet, or on a corporate intranet.

By eliminating some of the parts in a PC, manufacturers can sell these NCs for less than $1,000, considered a magic price-point. Companies like Oracle have bet hundreds of millions of dollars that NCs will capture a significant portion of the computer market.

The Bagel Effect predicts a different future for NCs. The NC is a step backward from the perspective of empowering consumers. It supports an asymmetric system in which a powerful server computer dominates less capable client computers. In effect, an NC is a glorified terminal with connectivity. In that sense, it is a throwback to mainframe client-server architecture, where the system administrator controls the user's environment.

One can therefore predict that NCs will not ultimately capture a significant portion of the personal computer market. There are business situations, however, for which there is little need for full-featured computers. For example, a stock brokerage firm might require brokers to use a single application most of the time. This core application should work the same for all brokers and should be easy and economical to update and support by the technical staff. NCs fill these requirements quite well.

On the other hand, the price of personal computers is dropping so rapidly that it is difficult to see why users would buy an intentionally crippled appliance that denies them control of their working environment. For example, Apple Computer has released the iMac, a very powerful computer complete with a hard disk drive, CD-ROM drive, Ethernet, high-speed modem, high-definition monitor, and standard operating system, for about $1,000 (US street price).

Computer Software

Computers are naturally interactive. You don't watch a computer, you operate it. You run software — programs, desk accessories, browsers, and games. In many ways, software and operating systems are causing the biggest changes in the computer industry. In this arena, the Bagel Effect is very evident.

Operating Systems

Let's start with operating systems. There are four major operating systems in use today: Windows, Windows NT, Mac OS, and UNIX. In order to compete, they have all acquired graphic interfaces, the ability to run many programs at the same time (multi-tasking), and the ability to display moving pictures. These and other features have made their size and complexity balloon. It is very difficult to test them thoroughly because of the variety of hardware and applications available for them. The operating systems crash frequently (more than once a day on average) and require lots of computer memory and disk storage in order to function as advertised.

Perhaps the biggest problem with operating systems is that application developers must decide either to have their program work on a single system or spend a great deal of time and money developing several versions, one for each system. Because these operating systems are non-interoperable, they are not Bagel-friendly.

Java

Sun Microsystems, one of the major computer manufacturers, developed a language called Java in an attempt to overcome some of these difficulties. It has been designed to run on all popular computers and under all operating systems. What this means is that you can use a Java application regardless of which hardware or operating system you have. This is a great boon for software developers because they can create a single application and sell it to the widest market. That lowers the development cost, increases the potential revenue, and ultimately lowers the price to consumers.

One of the attractive features of Java is that it allows small applications (applets, in Java terminology) to be downloaded from a network automatically when they are needed. Unlike previous methods of downloading software from network servers, Java protects the user's computer from unwanted tampering and security breaches. This user focus makes Java Bagel-friendly.

In order to establish Java as an industry standard, Sun has made its specifications and protocols public, and has encouraged a consortium of competing computer companies to collaborate on its development. Java could begin to erode the market domination of proprietary operating systems in the next few years. Some competitors to Sun have taken advantage of the Java open standard to create Java-compatible systems. Hewlett-Packard was able to develop its own version of Java, for instance, and this will add competition, increase Java's market penetration, and lower costs to consumers.

Thin Clients

Perhaps the most important implication of Java is that inexpensive NC computers can be made functional without the use of one of the major operating systems. So long as the NC's functionality can be limited to applications written in the Java language, it does not require the complexity or cost of an expensive operating system. Java applications can be run on a pared-down version of an operating system, known as a *thin client*.

Obviously, Java is seen as a big threat to Microsoft, the company that thrives on its sales of Windows, the most popular operating system. While Microsoft does everything it can to oppose the spread of Java, it must incorporate Java capability in its Windows system or lose customer support, because many applications are available only in Java.

Video Games

Companies like SONY, Nintendo, and Sega have sold more than 100 million video game machines throughout the world. These are just special-purpose computers. When you add this installed base to the number of computers sold, all of which can run video games, you begin to understand the staggering extent of interactive digital gaming. Games continue to be one of the essential software categories and have enlarged their initial audience of teenaged boys to encompass girls and adults.

Games are very Bagel-friendly because they are inherently interactive and personal. The distribution system for game software, however, has not yet succumbed to the Bagel Effect, because the major manufacturers use proprietary software and hardware systems. So, if you have a SONY Playstation and want to play Super Mario, you have to buy a second machine (from Nintendo). Consequently, games on computer CD-ROMs have gained market share because you can play all titles on your PC — you don't have to buy a stand-alone player from SONY, Nintendo, or Sega.

BAGEL BITS

You can buy third-party microchips to add functionality to some video games. One example is a RAM chip that allows a player to save the configuration of the game when it's shut down so you don't have to start from the beginning the next time you play.

Video games will increasingly allow third-party plug-ins to add more sophisticated functionality. If learning materials and school assignments were available as plug-ins, kids would have to complete their homework before continuing to the next play level. This might yield an acceptable balance for parents between Bagel Effect video-gaming, in which kids have all the control, and parental/institutional regulation.

Netscape Navigator

Netscape Navigator, one of the first Internet browser applications, was the key element that popularized the Internet. Every aspect of the browser and the company that produced it was in line with the Bagel Effect.

Mark Andreesen, Netscape's co-founder, was an undergraduate at University of Illinois at Urbana when he helped develop a free Internet browser called Mosaic. A few years later he left university and founded Netscape with former Silicon Graphics chief Jim Clark. Netscape parlayed a free Internet browser into one of the biggest business launches this century. Founded in April 1994 with no significant sales, Netscape went public a year later on August 9, 1995. Demand for the stock was so high that the initial offering had to be increased from 2.5 million shares to 5 million shares and the offering price was raised from $14 to $28. That's a 400% increase in value before the offering hit the street. The initial capitalization was $3 billion, but by the end of 1995, NetScape stock had risen to $7 billion.

What was it about Netscape's business plan that caught everyone's imagination? Why did David Menlow, president of the IPO Financial Network, say, "It's a singular situation and shouldn't be confused for any frothiness in the market or excessive tendencies of investors"? Here's the gist of Netscape's plan:

- Create a browser for the World Wide Web;
- Give it away free (or bundle it for almost free);
- Let anyone download it from your Web site;
- Sell advertising on your Web site;
- Sell server software to Web site operators so they can reach the millions of Netscape browser users.

Within months of going public the media was taking bets on whether Netscape's vision of the future — an Internet browser with plug-in applications for word processing and other functions — or Microsoft's vision of the future — an operating system with a built-in Internet browser — would dominate the next century. The most incredible aspect of this story is that Netscape, a company with no history and only a few months on the stock market, was vying with industry Goliath Microsoft.

Whatever the final outcome of the browser wars, the early success of Netscape was due to recognition that the new power base lay outside the networks, in the hands of end users: Hook the users and you've got a valuable bargaining chip. The following characteristics of Netscape Navigator are also defining elements of the Bagel effect:

- Users, not the Web page designers, control the fonts, colors, and other design elements.

- Users can get the browser anywhere (stores, on the Web) either free or nearly free.

- The computer source code is available (free) to users and developers.

- Navigator is available for all major computers.

- Navigator doesn't control the user's environment. It accepts third-party plug-ins in a standard format. They range from spreadsheets to movie and music players, greatly enhancing its utility.

- Users can customize Netscape to have as many features as they need.

- Navigator was the first browser to incorporate Java, allowing thousands of programmers around the world to write applications that are guaranteed to work on any computer running Navigator.

Application Programs

Computer programs, like operating systems, have become bloated. In a race to add more and more functionality within each application, they have become huge, slow, difficult to configure, and more complicated to use. This trend shows no signs of slowing or reversing unless software designers adopt a drastically different approach to programming. Such a new approach has been growing steadily over the past decade. It's called object-oriented programming.

In traditional computer languages like Basic, or C, a programming team creates an application by designing all the functions into the main program, breaking it down into parts called routines and subroutines. All the program parts are compiled into the final program using a complicated procedure that checks each part for the computer resources it needs for execution, and for the communication it must have with other parts. If you want to create a new application, you more or less design it from scratch because the parts that worked in a previously written program can not integrate with parts in the new program.

I used to write computer programs. I worked on teams that created music processors called sequencers, which let you create and play music on a computer. Each program required the creation of a basic music player; a difficult and time-consuming task. It was created and compiled into one program, but it was not usable in another program compiled to run on a different computer or under a different operating system.

Don't Object to Objects

Object-oriented programs, on the other hand, are based on small, reusable parts called objects. Instead of the programmer keeping all the power, control, and knowledge, software objects can contain a lot of information about themselves. A software object may know about its color, the way it creates an image on a screen, the way it processes text that is fed to it, and the way it can interact with other objects. Because it has not only a function but also instructions about how to interact with other objects, these instructions can be assembled in the user's computer instead of being compiled by the programmer.

An important advantage of object-oriented programming is that once you've created an object that has a function, that object may be placed in a library and assembled into other programs. In the example I used earlier, a music player written in object code could be used any time a user wanted to play music, whether it was within a word processor or a slide-show program.

Object-oriented programming makes it possible to create toolkits of functionality that users can assemble to make their own application. The user then has control of the functionality, as many or as few features as required. In order to accomplish this, software designers must develop object-oriented software components.

Software Components

Software component architecture takes the object concept a step further. Users can manipulate software components instead of programmers. They are therefore *very* Bagel-friendly and may well change the face of computing over the next decade. Here's how they work.

Let's say your word-processing needs are generally simple. You need to write and read correspondence that's mostly e-mail. You don't write technical manuals, you don't put spoken notes into your documents, and you don't create videos that play when someone opens your document. You don't work on documents with others who need to mark their revisions in different colors and you don't need a glossary of boilerplate clauses that you insert into legal documents. You don't need to create fancy artwork and integrate it into your document. All of these capabilities and many others are found in today's full-featured word processors like Microsoft's Word or Corel's Word Perfect. All users pay for these features. All users suffer the consequences of huge memory and disk requirements and, worst of all, application instability.

With component architecture, you might buy an inexpensive, bare-bones word processor. It may work perfectly well for you until the day you have to write an important proposal and need a spelling checker. On that day, with component architecture, you could take a spelling checker component and place its icon on the icon of your document. Voilà! You can now spell-check your document. You may have only purchased the rights to use the spelling checker for a few days or you may have purchased a blanket right to automatically download component architecture modules from the Web for a yearly fee. The point is, you get and pay for the basic functions you need. You can get more functionality when you need it, under terms and conditions suitable to you.

Applets

In this new vision of user-centered application assembly, someone might create a Java component — an applet — to play music (following our earlier example). The applet would be immediately usable by those wanting to listen to background music while working on their computers. The applet could also function within a word processor or while browsing a Web site, on a Mac, a PC, or a UNIX computer.

The implications don't stop there. If a telephone equipment manufacturer wanted to put music functionality into a telephone they could use the music player applet. It could also be used on a personal digital assistant or a hand-held calculator. Just as convergence is enabling many industries and media to use the same interoperable digital formats, component architecture promises to bring interoperability to software-driven industries, cheaply and quickly.

Try to imagine the implications for a small software company. Up until now, it would pick a single platform, target a single operating system, and then create a game or productivity program that it hoped would be successful. It would be able to afford porting the application to other platforms and operating systems only if the software was a hit. Even if it was a hit, the small company would be competing with the muscle of the Microsofts of the world.

Now imagine the same company operating in a component-architecture environment. Instead of producing a game, it might take an existing game written in a component architecture, perhaps a successor to Super Mario, and add a new function, new characters, and so on. Nintendo still gets the basic software and hardware sale but our small company gets to add value for the user and at the same time play in the same arena as the big guys.

BAGEL BITS

Falling prices, LAN connectivity in your home, just-in-time applets, and user-assembled software will make computers as ubiquitous as telephones. Most important, you can look forward to simpler computer systems in which you will be able to place as much or as little functionality as you need and want to pay for.

Perhaps the best bellwether for computing in the next millennium comes from Xerox PARC (Palo Alto Research Center), the folks who, among other things, invented the graphic user interface now used by both Apple OS and Microsoft Windows. John Seely Brown of Xerox calls the next big advance **calm computing.**

Calm computing is the result of computer technology maturing and becoming invisible. It is like "calm" writing with a ballpoint pen — you never have to think about the technology behind the pen, you just pick it up and write. The idea is to get the technology and interface out of the user's consciousness by designing computers that are transparent to the tasks at hand. At its root, calm computing is in sync with the Bagel Effect because it gives the user freedom and control over what he or she wants to do.

17 TELEPHONY
Dialing for Dollars

"We are hearing ... that the Internet could swallow not only telephony but all of telecommunications. A few people are beginning to talk about traditional telephone service having only a three to five year life span left."

— *The COOK Report* published on the Internet, January 12, 1998, by COOK Network Consults, Ewing, N.J., www.cookreport.com/building.html

In 1993 Stewart Verge, vice president of Bell Canada Networks, said, "We've been shocked by the introduction of cellular technology, which changed our paradigm that communication takes place over wires between fixed locations. Now we realize that communication takes place between people — people on the move."

Verge articulated a fundamental problem facing telcos. Until now, they have understood their business as encompassing the telephone network and appliances. But communications isn't about a network and wires, it's about people sending and receiving messages — system inputs and outputs at the edges, in Bagel Effect parlance. Some of these messages are spoken and some are electronic data like fax and computer files. We speak of telephony today as encompassing all messages, and frequently, there are no telephones at all in the communication link.

Freedom of Movement

One of the Bagel Effects in telephony is that service will take place where users want it, not where it's convenient for suppliers. *Star Trek* fans have known for decades that the future will bring a communicator worn as an accessory to clothing. This bit of science-fiction prognostication is reasonable because the device is convenient for the user, and we are quickly moving into a world in which the user, not the provider, will determine the success of products.

Nearly everything we previously did with wires can now be done without them. Wireless and cellphones are replacing tethered telephones at such a fast pace that the cellular system has been unable to cope with the traffic. The appeal of cellphones was so underestimated that a mere five years after their introduction the entire system needed replacement. This massive shift was not predicted by the telephone industry, but is entirely in keeping with the Bagel Effect, which predicts freedom will win out over central control.

Why did the phone companies get it wrong? They had a captive market in which customers were forced to come to their appliances for service. Since everyone used the telephone service, the telcos assumed that consumers were happy with their product. But consumers had never been given a choice. Once they were allowed to choose between freedom of movement versus location-controlled access, they went with Bagel choice.

The cell phone explosion raises the question of where the focus of telephony should be placed. The high concept of telephony is, of course, the user appliance we know as the telephone. It is a portal to communications. It has hardly changed in the past hundred years. The form and function of phones were so well designed that today's cellphones and the handsets of the 1920s are easily identified as the same basic appliance. Communication takes place between people. So long as the telephone remained the focus of attention it was natural to keep users at the forefront of the industry's thinking.

But the biggest changes in telephony over the past fifty years have been network-focused, and that has bred the problematic corporate culture in telcos today. So much of the business has evolved around network services that executives have forgotten the basis of their business — communications and end users.

If the telephone industry is not to repeat its mistakes of underestimating the popularity of wireless phones and the Internet, it will have to refocus on customers and heed the Bagel Effects that are driving change in the industry.

WANs and LANs

The telecommunications networks are undergoing a transformation that is making them look more like LANs than traditional telephone WANs. LANs are relatively passive networks in which data packets have addresses attached to them and find their destinations using protocols like Ethernet. WANs have traditionally dealt with switched circuits in which the telephony data have no minds of their own but travel down paths switched by the telco equipment to provide end-to-end continuity.

The complexity and control of WANs have been concentrated in large central offices — COs — each of which switched an entire region of telephone calls. All calls beginning with a certain area code and the initial three digits of an exchange would go to a single central office for switching. The newer technologies introduce packet-switching technologies, in which many conversations and lots more data travel down the same pathways, wrapped with information headers that describe their destinations. The fiber-optic digital networks are connected to digital routers, which read the destination headers and route each packet along paths that will get them to their destinations. These new routers are more numerous than the central office switches and have much more intelligence. They are located throughout exchanges at the edges of the network, close to users.

This is a clear migration of network power and control to the edges of the system, a Bagel indicator. In this sense, telephony is moving towards architectures that more closely resemble the Internet, shifting emphasis away from the central offices and away from the control of telco planners. Whereas it was difficult for third parties to control traffic on WANs when the telcos controlled the switches, routers are interoperable devices that enable third parties to easily interoperate with the telephony networks, weakening their monopolistic hold on the traffic.

Local and Long-Distance

The concepts of local and long-distance telephone service are out of date now that digital connectivity has turned the world into a global village. When telephones first came into general use, the cost of long-distance calls was high, so people would go to great lengths to arrange that the person they were calling would be available at the other end. It was not unusual to send letters in advance to relatives and business associates asking that they be near their telephones on a certain date at a certain time so that long-distance charges would not be wasted. Indeed, the original long-distance trunk lines were scarce resources that had to be carefully managed.

By the '50s, when I was growing up, the telephone companies had made available person-to-person rates so that you didn't have to pay for a call unless you reached your intended party at the other end. But the cost for these calls was even higher than normal long-distance. I remember members of my family arranging verbal codes to save long-distance charges. When I arrived safely at summer camp, say, I phoned home person-to-person and asked for myself. My parents would say no, I wasn't home, there would be no charge for the call, and they would know I arrived safely at my destination. I remember feeling guilty about cheating the telephone companies, at the time.

How times have changed! Today, family members routinely exchange calls with their relatives around the globe with little thought for the cost. The competitive rates for long-distance calls now are settling at about ten cents per minute no matter where you call. This is less than the local rate for using a cellphone. Therefore, the user sees no great distinction between local and long-distance calling.

Telephony providers, on the other hand, see these two businesses as distinct and separate, due to the way their industry has been regulated by governments. Because governments first deregulated the long-distance business, a competitive infrastructure has grown up in that area. Local telephone rates are beginning their cycle of deregulation but are still kept artificially low to ensure that all residents can have basic service at an affordable rate. This subsidization of local rates is paid for by long-distance suppliers, but is being phased out, as local telephony becomes market-driven.

Numbered for Life

The Bagel Effect encourages users to be in direct control of their telecommunications services. The number-one demand from consumers is a permanent telephone number that will follow them when they move, whether they are at home or at the office, whether they pick up a tethered phone, a cellphone, or a messaging service. In order to accommodate their customers, service providers will have to make arrangements with each other and develop technologies to keep the service simple from the user's perspective. Telecommunications suppliers will have to accommodate these and other users' needs of their customers if they are to win their business in a newly competitive environment.

Rates

We used to pay for telephone calls according to how far away the other connection was and how long the call lasted — distance and time. Most phone rates were very complex, varying by time of day, day of the week, and destination area code. But phone rates have plunged precipitously and rate structures have become greatly simplified because:

- Digital switching has reduced the cost of operating networks;
- Fiber-optic networks have greatly increased capacity compared to copper wires;
- Deregulation has fostered fierce competition;
- The Internet model of fixed monthly pricing provides an attractive alternative for consumers;
- Computer networks have converged with telco networks.

These are results of the Bagel Effect.

Today, you can buy long-distance services at a flat rate, without regard to how far away the destination is. We are now seeing the introduction of fixed monthly rates, no matter how many long-distance calls you make — the Internet pricing model. Thus, the business is moving towards a flat connectivity cost, a price for bandwidth access.

A Commodity Business

This leads to predictions that the telco network itself will cease to produce the profit levels it once did. As competing fiber-optic networks become available from many suppliers, the business of carrying signals will become a commodity low-margin business, to the consumer's benefit. The trend that we have seen in long-distance, where a new supplier eager to gain market share undercuts the market pricing, will continue.

The telcos and other bandwidth suppliers see this coming. They realize that the only road to higher margins will be added services that distinguish one carrier from another. These new services are already beginning to blossom. In addition to permanent phone numbers, suppliers are offering voice recognition for dialing and information, personal telephone directories, voice messaging, and caller identification. Coming soon will be content-based services like booking theater tickets, weather reports, sports scores, news and entertainment.

Telephony Without Voices

Not so long ago the focus of telephone companies was on carrying the human voice. Audio quality, acceptable time delays for two-way conversations, and other technical issues were approached with the assumption that people would be having voice conversations on telephone lines. But voice is no longer the predominant traffic carried by telcos today.

For the first time, data traffic is eclipsing traditional voice traffic. As information continues to explode and voice traffic stays static, voice will become a relatively insignificant portion of telephony. By 2002, voice is expected to be less than 1% of telecom traffic.

Susan Almeida, in her article "Voice and Data Worlds Collide," supports the Bagel Effect arguments when she says:

> Explosive data growth and voice [traffic migrating to the Internet] are fundamentally altering the global telecom infrastructure. The shift from traditional [telephone] networks to [Internet-like] data-centric networks is more fundamental than the last great transition from analog to digital. That shift created economic activity measuring billions of dollars ... Today's sea change from circuit-switched to packet-switched nets will make that transition look like

child's play. In the wake of this great re-build, some very big players too slow to move will be shunted to walking-dead status; others with the innovation and courage to act will be catapulted to the head of the race.

Just the FAX

Faxes already accounts for 40% of all telephony. Fax traffic is a natural migrant to the Internet because it does not require the same quality of service as voice conversations; a fax transmission can pause for a second if necessary without disturbing the transmission. And when fax business leaves the telephone networks, they will lose almost half their traffic. Businesses have already started to use the Internet because they save all the long-distance charges on out-of-town faxes. New-model fax machines can be connected either to normal telephone lines or through Internet interfaces built into the machines.

Internet Access Providers

The biggest growth area is Internet access. Canadian telcos began offering their Sympatico brand of Internet access in 1996, and by the end of 1998, it had captured the lion's share of the business with 400,000 subscribers. At twenty dollars a month, that's $96 million of annual cash. This is still a pittance compared to total communications activities, but it's a good start.

One expects that in the future telcos will use their natural advantage of having a local subscriber base to offer combined local, long-distance, and digital network services with discounts for customers who subscribe to more than one.

The convergence of cable TV services and telephone services is allowing the telcos to deliver broadcast cable TV, beginning in late 1998. But, as in the phone business, competition will drive cable television to a low-margin business as prices to the consumer drop significantly.

Phone Service from Your Cableco

The biggest change for cablecos is that they will begin to offer telephony services. This has already begun in the United States and has been authorized in Canada. The major obstacle has been that the business doesn't appear to be very profitable because of the historic and artificially low local phone rates, which have been subsidized by long-distance income. As these subsidies are removed and market forces come into play, the cablecos and others will join in as suppliers.

When it comes to the Internet and its intranet successors, the cablecos have already begun to compete with telcos. In Canada, Rogers, Shaw, and Cogico, who between them account for most of the cable subscribers in Canada, have launched a new high speed Internet service called @Home.Canada. This service already boasts an estimated 100,000 subscribers by the end of 1998, with a long list of customers waiting to be connected.

Different Strokes

Suppliers of bandwidth like telcos and cablecos will have to differentiate their services in order to attract new customers. They will have to sell unique services like entertainment and educational courses that can't be compared to their competitors' offerings. To do so, they will agree to pay premium prices for specialty services if they can be acquired on an exclusive basis. Intranet services like America On-line already compete for subscribers in this manner.

To overcome the Bagel trend of customers' evaporating loyalty to suppliers, telcos and other businesses will have to deliver significantly more than just price-competitive services. They will have to solve problems for and become personally involved with customers if they are to get their business.

Miramichi

In May 1997, I met Brad McNeill, General Manager of NBTel's Miramichi region in New Brunswick. When I asked him who his largest client was, he told me it was the local paper mill. I remarked that a paper mill didn't seem a likely candidate for the most telephony. How many phone calls could they make? Then he explained that telephone service was only part of his telco's offerings. Because the mill is a good customer, the telco also arranges for walkie-talkies and other communications services that the mill needs.

These are not typical telco services, and must be subcontracted from third parties. This executive received the Bagel Effect message loud and clear. The telco changed its business model from being supplier-focused to customer-focused. No longer do they ask customers, "Which of our services do you want?" but instead ask, "What can we do for you?" Miramichi Telephone expects that when phone competition becomes a factor in their business they will retain their customers because they will be competing on more than just the cost of bandwidth. This is the recipe for success in the Bagel Effect years.

Symmetry Is Important

Many new added-value opportunities will come when broadband services become available. Broadband simply means that the pipeline to your home or office is big enough to deliver smooth video and high-fidelity audio. Users will pay for music-on-demand, movies-on-demand, television programs-on-demand, CD-ROMs-on-demand, learning-on-demand, and videophone access to doctors, veterinarians, and other professionals.

Digital infrastructure designers need to know how much content will originate with a user in order to engineer the most efficient and effective networks. They need to know whether people will use the new digital networks to send each other home movies, or if they will be satisfied with only receiving movies from the Hollywood producers. The first scenario requires a symmetrical network in which the end users can also be providers of content. The second scenario is asymmetric where more information travels in one direction than in the other. Mass communication systems like newspapers and television are asymmetric. A television program goes from the broadcaster to a passive viewer with no provision for flow in the other direction.

In contrast, telephone networks are symmetric. They allow users to send information from any point of presence on the network to any other. Symmetrical systems, such as the telephone network, allow for the same bandwidth in both directions — you can speak and listen with the same fidelity. Symmetrical systems are required for videophones since communication can originate with any user. Natural human conversation uses our eyes, ears, vocal chords, mouths, gestures, and neural processing systems that enable us to send and receive information at the same time. The Bagel Effect suggests that as users gain control of their communications systems, they will want them to mimic their biological communications systems: they will want full-fidelity — broadband — and two-way — symmetrical — networks.

Read My Lips

The directors of Western Union, the communications giant in the age of telegraphy, passed judgment on telephone technology in 1876 when they concluded that "the device is inherently of no value to us." Clearly, some devices are ahead of their time because their utility has not yet been established. Today, similar comments are being made about videophones. Like telephones a hundred years ago, videophones will become ubiquitous within the next fifty years. No one will have to make a business case for them because no one will dream of doing without them.

Ever since science fiction movies like *2001* and *Star Trek* began portraying video telephones as normal everyday appliances, the public has accepted the concept and assumed that, in time, the bulk of our communications will include visual as well as audio information. Up until now, however, attempts to market videophones have fizzled.

These failures should not be taken as a sign that video telephony isn't commercially viable, only that the product introductions have had fatal flaws. First and foremost, without a critical mass of connected users, the value of any sort of telephony is very low. For business, you need to have your key staff and/or customers on-line. At home you need to have your friends and relatives available. These are bare minimums. Critical mass never takes place without industry standards and low entry price-points. These requirements have not yet been met, and so videophones haven't had a fair crack at the market.

On the technical side, the telephone networks and the Internet have not yet offered the bandwidth to deliver any video except small, jerky images, resembling more a succession of stills than true-motion video. These images are inadequate to convey the gestural information we need for natural visual communication.

In 1994, CulTech Research Centre ran a trial at York University in which we wired Calumet College, a student residence, with videophones. One hundred students had videophones in their dormitories. Although they couldn't communicate with the outside world, they could contact each other. We tested many factors, including the need for visual privacy, the quality of the visual image, the frame rate necessary for comfortable visual communications, and so on. What we found was very interesting.

The size and quality of the image were important but not critical issues. The frame rate, however, was a key factor in whether the students found the videophones useful. Slow, jerky motion in the images broke the perceptual flow of the conversations. This explains why some of the products offered by telephone companies like AT&T have failed. Another key factor was the user interface. Computer-like interfaces with pull-down menus and many settings were a turn-off. Users are accustomed to the simple, direct interface of a telephone and want no less from their videophones.

After we designed a simple interface and brought the frame rate up to about fifteen frames a second the system received a surprisingly high volume of use. Because it was a digital, computer-based system, we were able to include voicemail without much difficulty or cost. This allowed students to call each other, to arrange for collaborating on school projects or to make a date to see a movie. Although the dormitories were only a few hundred yards apart, students used their videophones frequently to communicate.

The next-generation videophones were deployed in the Intercom Ontario trial for the Stonehaven West community in 1997. The biggest impediment to use in this suburb is simply that there are not enough users connected with common interests. Unlike the student trial, the residents are a less homogeneous sample, and are frequently not at home when neighbors call. Nonetheless, they are using the videophones for hiring local babysitters (they like looking a first-time sitter in the eye), inviting friends over for a barbecue, and so on. Most of the use is by kids, who have the time to call many friends until they find one who's at home and ready to chat.

The results are very encouraging but emphasize the need for a sizeable group of users with videophones so callers have enough choice of people to talk to. The same held true for fax, which was viewed as a business gadget until a worldwide standard was settled on and enough companies bought fax machines to enable useful interactions. Video telephony is on the brink of exploding. It will do so when broadband networks reach significant penetrations because at that point the incremental cost of adding video will be small, perhaps no more than a one time fee of $100.

BAGEL BITS

The gender differentiation was different than what we expected in the Calumet College videophone trial. The average length of a videomail message was twice as long for male students as for female students. So much for women being more talkative than men. On the other hand, women were more likely to turn off the video portion of the system than men were, perhaps because they were more concerned about their appearance than men. Both sexes were uncomfortable with having video cameras in their dorms and frequently placed a hat or other covering item on the camera, even when it was turned off.

Alex, the Telco Visionary

Alexander Graham Bell invented the telephone to help hard-of-hearing people communicate but he believed its commercial value would be in the entertainment field. He envisaged bringing concert music to a greater public than could fit into a concert hall. He wrote about having one telephone in Carnegie Hall and other telephones connected by a network to homes throughout New York City. People would be able to enjoy concerts in the comfort of their homes. They would pay to hear Enrico Caruso singing in their homes. It didn't occur to Alex that person-to-person communications would become the most valuable commercial use of the telephone network.

Today, as in the last century, the powerful movers and shakers don't believe that personal communications will be the killer application for networks. Somehow the thought of putting people in touch seems too socially redeeming to be a big money-maker. Marketers echo the previous century's seers who predicted that new networks would profit primarily from the delivery of entertainment. But people are social and like to communicate with each other. They do this for business, to learn, and for fun. The future for telephony is bright but only those organizations that understand human communications and the over-riding Bagel Effect will prosper. Get rid of those engineers and hire some sociologists!

18 NEW MEDIA
Digital and Interactive

What the heck are new media and just how new are they? There is not always agreement about what constitutes the new media. Until recently governments were using the terminology *new media* and *telematics* to describe the field, although I have never met anyone outside of government who knows what telematics is.

The new media are digital and interactive. These include CD-ROMs and the Internet but would exclude music CDs, which are digital but not interactive. At some point these media will cease being new and so the term will not last long. A more descriptive name would simply be digital interactive media, but for this chapter we'll stick to current usage.

In March 1998, I was at a roundtable discussion about new media with Canada's Ministers for Heritage and Industry, at which industry representatives were asked to explain our views on the future of new media. The answers ranged from SchoolNet — connecting all Canadian schools together via the Internet — to software for Nintendo and Sega video games. A more appropriate way to look at new media is that they will be the interactive digital mediation through which all types of education, information, entertainment, and communications will take place.

Multimedia

The buzzword a few years ago was *multimedia*. Multimedia described the incorporation of text, images, animations, sound, and videos in a single product. The products available then were computer programs. Some were delivered on floppy disks and some were delivered on CD-ROMs.

That name became troublesome because other products combined many media types too. After all, movies can incorporate all of these elements, as can television. And Web sites, which fit the description, were not included in the industrial use of the term. So *multimedia*, like *distance education*, has fallen into disuse.

Interactive Media

Interactive media is a better description of the field than *multimedia* because it focuses on the element that has changed the way content is being produced. The word interactive clearly excludes television and movies.

Unfortunately, though videodiscs are interactive and encompass many media, they are not included in the new media because they are not digital. As analog relics, they cannot interoperate on the levels of data, format, or media with the new digital systems. As a result, they are being marginalized and will vanish completely, as digital videodiscs — DVD — quickly replace them.

So we're back to speaking of *new media*. Here's what we're talking about.

CD-ROM

The first category of new media is CD-ROM. The chapters on media (in Part IV), digitization (Chapter 7), and interactivity (Chapter 9) describe CD-ROMs from those perspectives. CD-ROMs actually represent a wide variety of products based on optical laser technology that creates and recognizes tiny pits in the plastic that correspond to the digital 1s and 0s of the binary number system.

CD-ROMs come in many flavors ranging from read-only disks that you buy in a software store, to writable disks that allow the user to store and retrieve information at will. CD-ROMs are increasingly popular because of their low cost. You can store a gigabyte of information on a writable disc for less than two dollars.

The original CD-ROMs were slow by computer standards. They could transfer data at about 150 kilobytes a second compared to magnetic media such as hard disks that can transfer data at about fifty times that rate.

As the technology of CD-ROMs improved, players have been able to read the information much more quickly. The original players are now referred to as 1X players, with newer, more capable machines designated as 2X, and so on. 24X players are available now and they can transfer data almost as fast as hard disks.

Networks

The other half of the new media equation involves digital networks. When these use Internet-like protocols (IP) they qualify as both digital and interactive. The interactivity is generally from hyperlinks (see Chapter 9, Interactivity) so one may say that these networks are "hyperactive." The great benefit of networks is that you pay a one-time-only fee to store data on a server, since no copies are physically distributed. Whenever you want to access a file or product, you can do so over the network without the need to store the information permanently on your computer.

Broadcast and New Media

Television production is a mature and profitable industry in Canada. Support mechanisms are in place to encourage new projects and productions and these have been successful in building an industry that competes internationally and sells its products and services in Canada and abroad. Support takes the form of public funds like Telefilm Canada and the provincial government agencies, as well as private funds like the Canadian Television and Cable Production Fund, which is supported by a percentage of cable fees from subscribers.

When it comes to interactive projects, whether multimedia or on-line, there has been very little financial support available. Since the telcos need this type of content to add value to their broadband services, they decided to set up new funds, such as the Bell Broadcast and New Media Fund, that parallel the objectives of the established broadcast funds. The telcos need interactive products if they are to differentiate their wares from traditional broadcast television, and they need to score brownie points with the federal CRTC regulator as they begin to compete with cablecos in the regulated cable television market.

A few years ago, CulTech Research Centre began hosting annual conferences in order to try to bridge the gap between the broadcast and new media industries. The first conference was InterActive '96. InterActive featured workshops for TV and film people to acquaint them with the terms and technologies of interactive media. The conference itself, with Buffy Sainte-Marie as our keynote speaker, dealt with thorny issues like intellectual property ownership in collaborative teams, and the loss of creative control in interactive writing.

It was a step in the right direction. There is good reason to integrate Canada's multimedia industries. As a relatively small country with insufficient markets to sustain a production industry without foreign sales, we need to marshal our strengths to produce world-class content. For the same reason, when I was Chairman of the Academy of Canadian Cinema in 1982, I expanded the Academy's film focus to include television. The expanded Academy of Canadian

Cinema and Television now produces the Gemini Awards, the Prix Gémeaux, and the Genie Awards and has enough stability from the combined production communities to carry it through the inevitable periods of crisis.

BellFund

One of the new funds that I chair, the Bell Broadcast and New Media Fund — BellFund — was established in July 1997 to encourage television producers to partner with new media producers. The concept is to use the strong and well-developed television industry to promote new media productions, while bringing the interactive digital expertise of new media producers to augment the television products. The BellFund is distributing $12 million to qualifying productions.

We hope to bring the two solitudes of broadcast television and digital interactive media together. At first glance, this seems a bit like a shotgun marriage, but on further examination, it makes some sense. The television industry has a broad business infrastructure, publicly traded companies, and lots of money. Canada is the second largest supplier of television content in the world. But broadcasters look down at the new media because in their view it is not ready for prime time, without a mass market of "eyeballs" to sell to advertisers. Broadcasters have no experience with digital or interactive projects and have little understanding of how to create them. They do have viable models for making money on broadcast networks.

New media professionals, on the other hand, know everything that is now known about how to create products for digital networks and interactive media. But they are grossly underfunded and do not have viable business models for making money on digital networks.

Each of these media has advantages that we hope can be used in synergy. Broadcast has the suppliers and advertisers. It can deliver a mass market not only for programs but also for marketers and promoters. New media bring narrowcast markets to suppliers but, more important, deliver user choice, which drives new business. The objective is to couple television programs with associated new media promoted by the broadcasters. Viewers tune into the linear program to establish the story, characters, or other themes and then get individual attention and control through the new media. A new medium might be, for example, a Web site, but not just a promotional site for the TV program.

BAGEL BITS

Riverdale is a CBC prime-time soap. The producer, Linda Schuyler, partnered with new media producer Raja Khanna of Snap Media to develop a cyber-soap that's available on the Web. The Web site takes you behind the scenes to follow the crew as they make the television program. You get to learn about what a gaffer does, what a director of cinematography does and so on. The kicker is that the crew characters are themselves embroiled in a soap opera of plots and subplots. You get the name-brand recognition of the series that brings you to the Web site (promoted on television), plus you get to follow the plot line of your choice — relationships among the crew and main characters.

Is this the future of television? Is this the future of new media? Unlikely. Does it point to probable directions for the new media and television industries? Quite possibly. The intriguing concept is the marriage of linear and interactive media in a manner that maximizes the strengths of each medium. One of the outcomes has already been made clear. If you put some significant money on the table, people will find a way to access it, even if it means restructuring their creative and business relationships. After less than a year of operation, the BellFund has gone from funding every qualifying application (in the first six months) to funding only one out of five because of the volume and quality of projects.

User as Moviemaker

I visited the Broad Alliance for Multimedia Technology and Applications in Silicon Valley south of San Francisco. They used a grant from NASA to develop and deliver broadband content on a trial basis. One of their projects set up a community facility where people could learn to use computer tools for making interactive multimedia stories about themselves — sort of the next step for home movies. I was taken with the incredibly personal nature of what the participants created, and how, taken as a whole, it gave me a wonderful window into that particular community.

One middle-aged woman had a best friend she'd known since they were five years old. She and her friend had kept scrapbooks of their activities together, along with some home movies. The women always thought their relationship was like Lucy Ricardo and Ethel Mertz's from the *I Love Lucy* TV series. The woman surfed the Web, found a host of *I Love Lucy* pictures and articles, and used them to link her own material along with some hilarious narrative.

A young man from Brooklyn had come to California because of a lucrative job offer but had left his wife and four children on the East Coast until he could determine whether California was a suitable permanent residence for them. He was very lonely and missed his family. His story was extremely personal and moving.

Another woman was a Holocaust survivor who had never been able to articulate her experiences in person. Interactive media allowed her to unburden herself for the first time in her life and, in the process, inform the community about what it was like in a concentration camp.

None of these stories warranted an hour of prime-time television. However, they were riveting for me, and I imagine they would be more so for the people in their community. Projects such as this will stimulate passive television audiences to become creators of their own content. As control moves from the few to the many, we will see an enormous outpouring of creativity, and a considerable fraction will be of interest to others, although the audiences may be very small.

PART 5
MESSAGES

Content Will Drives Economies

The messages that pass through the media are frequently labeled as communications, information, entertainment, or culture. Communications has been examined in broadcasting (Chapter 14), telephony (Chapter 17), and new media (Chapter 18). This section will concentrate on information, entertainment, and culture, which don't comfortably fit in the other categories.

In the telecommunications industry all message categories excluding communications are lumped together as *content*. It is generally acknowledged that content will drive the global economy of the next century as surely as raw materials and manufacturing drove the economy of this century.

The new cornucopia of content must be indexed and described, so individual items of interest may be linked with each other at the user's terminal. Internet search engines like *Yahoo* perform a simple version of this linking today. Finding commonality in disparate content will expose us to a wider horizon of relationships, and will help heal the plague of overspecialization that we've been suffering from.

ΒΑGΕL ΒΙΤS

There is evidence that information is being increasingly applied across unrelated fields. For example, mathematical chaos theory is used by hydrodynamicists building waterways, meteorologists predicting the weather, sociologists analyzing population growth, botanists studying plant forms, computer-graphic designers, and stockbrokers predicting market trends.

We are leaving the age of specialization and entering a new age in which the generalist with a passing knowledge of many fields will have the resources necessary to solve problems. These generalists will have knowledge that is broad in scope but shallow in detail, as opposed to today's specialists whose knowledge is narrow but deep.

The following chapters examine content in the form of:

- Information;
- Entertainment;
- Culture and The Arts;
- Intellectual Property.

19 INFORMATION
The Third Wave

"There's a line in *Apocalypse Now* where Capt. Kurtz says, 'This is my nightmare, this is my dream.' That's what the growth of Usenet is ... the public discussion groups making up Usenet have multiplied to 50,000 [topics]. The flow of new posts [public messages] has rocketed to 900,000 per day ... enough to fill a 6-gigabyte hard disc every 24 hours."

— *Internet World*, March 2, 1998.

Alvin Toffler speaks of three waves of human technologies. The first wave was agriculture, the second was industrialization, and the third is information. Just as the industrial age produced more watches than there were people, the information age has brought an abundance of data that is overwhelming us. As the mountain grows, we must learn to extract usable knowledge from it or it will become an avalanche that buries us.

The sheer volume of information available to everyone on the Internet is driving the commercial value of all information down to zero. Databases that were very valuable just a few years ago have little value today because similar information can be accessed on the Internet for free. Value is increasingly residing in contextualizing the information — organizing and processing it.

In the '50s, Sergeant Joe Friday of the *Dragnet* television series insisted, "Just the facts, that's all we want ... Just the facts." Investigators today know that circumstances are at least as important as the facts. Motivations, links, and emotions contribute to the context that surrounds the facts and gives facts significant meaning.

Information is not the same as knowledge. Knowledge comes from applying contextual frames to information. A list of average rainfall in Japan over the past hundred years is not particularly useful. However, if you present the data in the context of the seven-year-cycle of El Niño climate changes, this   rainfall list can produce knowledge about the probability for a good rice crop in the coming year.

Wisdom, one of the common aspirations among cultures, is the accumulation of knowledge that can be applied in new contexts. This metaphoric application of knowledge gained in one framework to information available in a different framework allows us to survive and prosper. However, at the root of it all is the acquisition of a rich information base.

Information Up, Brain Steady

Bill Buxton, director of research for Alias Waveframe, brings a refreshingly clear view to the problem of information overload. In a lecture at the McLuhan program at the University of Toronto, he pointed out that while the volume of information is increasing exponentially, the brain's capacity for storing, organizing, and recalling the data remains fixed. The result is a widening gap between the increasing volume of information and the capacity of our brains.

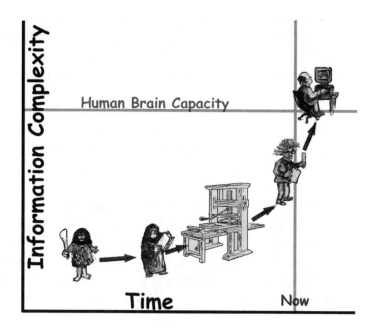

Figure 19.1 - The Brain Versus Information Complexity

For example, many computer programs are shipped with only a simple set-up booklet, while the full documentation, frequently hundreds of pages long, is available in a computer file. Very few users bother with the file-based information because it's too long and complex. Consequently, they only get to use a tiny fraction of the program's capability. The problem is not that the manual is too difficult to understand, it's that there are just too many manuals to digest and not enough time to do work and enjoy life.

Less Info, But On-Demand

Let's face it, the last thing we want is more information. Who wants more junk mail? Who wants more e-mail? Who needs to log onto half a million Internet sites? What we really want is *less* information. We want less mail, less e-mail, and fewer sites to visit in order to find what we want.

We *do* want control of our information. We want it to be drawn from the largest pool available, but filtered so we get only what we're interested in. The result would be a smaller volume of more manageable data. And we want that interesting fraction right away — on-demand.

The concept of on-demand information is congruent with the Bagel Effect because it puts control over the selection process and the delivery schedule in the hands of individual users. Info-on-demand is particularly well suited to networks where it has become a favorite among intranet and Internet users. Can't find the airline schedule? Check it out online. Looking for an image to paste into your presentation? Get one online from one of the free image databases. Need a sports score update? A sports Web site will give it to you along with profiles on all the players, the betting line at Vegas, and complete league statistics.

Commodity or Resource?

One of the contentious issues relating to the new wealth of information is its cost. Many believe that information — especially if it's been generated by public money — should be a resource shared by all and made available without fees. The Internet is a wonderful example of this principle in action. Until Web commerce began in the mid '90s, all information on the Internet was free.

On the other side of the argument are owners of valuable content who believe that information is a commodity like pork bellies, to be traded for market value. Hollywood movies, hit songs, popular books, newspaper databases, and private archives are examples of content that companies do not wish to make available without getting paid a fair return on their investments.

Like the Internet itself, information on digital networks is splitting into two segments: one that contains free resources and another that contains valuable marketable commodities.

In the years to come, there will be an increasingly large selection of free content, which will compete with commercial content. The end user will be the ultimate arbiter of value by deciding whether or not to pay for specific information, a concept consistent with the Bagel Effect.

BAGEL BITS

NASA — the space agency — makes large collections of scientific and historical images available without charge or restricted use. Many information services such as the **On-line Airline Guide** and the **New York Times** were first made available as fee-based services. After a while, the same information became available for free on the Internet.

Info + Tech = InfoTech

The dissemination of information has been closely linked to communications technologies, such as writing, printing, telephony, radio, and television. New technologies like photocopying, fax and the Internet have similar empowering capabilities.

The next century is being touted as an age for knowledge workers in a knowledge economy. As ordinary people acquire more knowledge, the gap between the info-poor and the info-rich will diminish, shifting the balance of power not only between social and economic classes, but also between nations.

BAGEL BITS

Third-world villagers who may not even have telephones today will be connected to all the agricultural information in the world within the next decade. They will increase their literacy with on-line interactive teaching systems that make use of sound and images to reinforce learning. They will have the opportunity to communicate with others throughout the world in similar circumstances, and with others in very different circumstances.

Digital Libraries

Libraries and archives have begun to convert their resources to digital formats and acquire new material on CD-ROMs and computer disks. A single copy of a popular book somewhere on the library network might be sufficient to service all the interested readers. Consequently, it will be less costly to open and maintain a small community library, because licensing access to digital content is less costly than buying physical books. On the other hand, many libraries will lose clients who have on-line access to the same content at home or at work.

Local libraries will increasingly be seen more as community access sites for connectivity than as repositories of physical resources. They will be the locus of activity for community members who lack connectivity at home or at work, allowing them to fully participate in the information age. Rare books and other unique collections will become important differentiators among libraries whose core materials will converge, as new media become ubiquitous.

Information Managers

The need for experts to organize the plethora of available titles will explode. Librarians and archivists will gain new and critical positions as information managers. They will be needed to catalog the huge numbers of individual content objects in collections, and to help library users find what they're looking for.

Once collections go on-line, there will be a rush to access archives that have hitherto been unavailable because of their inconvenient location, fragility of materials, or insufficient staff to service users. Many collections, like the Vatican archives, will be made available to the public for the first time as a result of their digitization.

The position of Chief Information Officer (CIO) has already become one of the most powerful in a corporation. The information technology (IT) operations within organizations will continue to rise in importance, because of the increasing need for expert service and individualized quality information, delivered in a timely manner.

Museums and Galleries

Museums and galleries throughout the world have only tiny fractions of their collections cataloged and available to outsiders. One of the great challenges of the twenty-first century will be to catalog and index these institutions' collections in digital databases that will be made available to other museums and galleries.

The databases will contain multimedia information — images, voice annotations, and videos — along with the searchable text. Dinosaur skeletons that are scattered in backroom drawers of museums throughout the world will be assembled into complete creatures because archeologists will have access to pictures and three-dimensional images of fossils outside their institution's collections. Forged paintings will be uncovered by comparing images from many collections in different countries. And new scientific theories will be put forward as the world's data becomes easily accessible to theorists everywhere.

The public will be able to visit museums and galleries from their homes and schools. Collections online have already become a fact of net life, with key collections like that of the Louvre made available to netizens throughout the world. Today they are available in low-resolution catalog-quality formats. Soon, they will be on-line in high resolution, with details available by enlarging the images with the click of a mouse.

Virtual Museums

In May 1998, Francesca Von Habsburg, director of the ARCH foundation, sponsored a *Virtual Museums on the Internet* conference in Salzburg, Austria. I was invited, along with museum curators, artists, and technology experts, to examine the feasibility of presenting collections online. Francesca's interest in virtual museums stems from her personal experience with collected art. Her family amassed some of the most significant art and jewelry in the world and, as a child, she would roller skate through her own private gallery of Picassos and Van Goghs. When her family established the public Thyssen-Bornemisza Museum in 1992, they moved the paintings, sculptures, carvings, tapestries, and gold objects to Madrid, Spain and Francesca felt an initial sense of immense loss. This was followed by a sense of liberation and satisfaction because the art was now available to a much larger audience who would share its wealth of human emotions.

Today she and others are keenly interested in making the world's collections available to the largest possible audience using digital networks. Although the online experiences will not be as rich as the experience of visiting a gallery or museum, they will greatly increase the exposure of great masses of people to the arts and sciences. In addition, the virtual museums and galleries will act as a magnet to bring people into physical museums and galleries where they can fully experience the original objects in the context of curated collections.

Both audiences and institutions will gain from the changes. Early online museum and gallery Web sites have already expanded the reach of their collections and memberships beyond their physical territories. In addition, networks allow users to access collections when galleries are closed and for as long they wish. This is important in the area of education because students frequently do their homework after-hours.

Universities

Universities hold all sorts of important collections and new content is constantly generated in the form of course notes, articles, photographs, illustrations, sound recordings, videos, books, presentations, and so on. These institutions will be able to license this information for on-line access around the world and generate significant fees that will help offset their operating expenses. This will put those schools that have developed peaks of expertise at an advantage and will differentiate them from other institutions.

Course materials and information archives will be a bonanza for learners and dabblers who will be able to access education and training without registering in institution programs. One can imagine lectures by Robertson Davies and art by the Group of Seven reaching new and wider audiences as digital networks reach into our homes and offices.

Communities

There is an enormous wealth of information in local communities, towns, villages, and cities: marriage records, births, deaths, baptisms, old news accounts, and so on. These will gradually be made available online, a boon not only to researchers but to police departments, governments, scholars, novelists, and individuals looking for family roots. The indexing and making up of this information will have to be done locally where the knowledge and context exists, thus generating work at the edges of our governments and institutions.

Chris Miller of Berea College in Kentucky wrote in *MUSEUM-L Magazine,*

> We are a small college museum, focused on Appalachian history and located in a rural community. Almost every visitor who visits Gallery V, our virtual on-line gallery, would not have come to the museum in person ... There are people in Ecuador who are interested in Appalachian Culture who cannot come to our museum. For them, any encounter with the stuff is better than no encounter at all.

Marking Up Information

Databases are much more valuable when they are cataloged, annotated, and marked up with descriptive information. The Internet, an immense database, became much more popular when its data was contextualized with linkages among words, images, and Web pages as a result of the World Wide Web. The process of inserting these HTML links is a form of marking up information to make it more useful.

Information mark-up is not a new concept but has taken off recently as a result of networked databases. The field is generating many new jobs and job categories. Formerly the domain of librarians, archivists, and secretaries, marking up the vast array of content that will be digitized is a task that will take more than a century.

First the information has to be cataloged. We have all fallen victim to the misfiled document that can no longer be found, or the videotape placed on the wrong shelf at a video rental store. Many physical collections have had restricted access because archivists cannot trust users to refile the documents or objects they take out after they're finished with them.

If you're looking for the *Being Digital* book, is it in the business or computer section of the bookstore? When you're searching for a physical object it can only be in one location. Fortunately, digital content need not be relegated to a single spot on the shelf. It may be simultaneously filed in many locations at the same time and will be found when searched for by any of its indexed attributes. So, in our example, you can find the digital book in both the business and computer sections.

BAGEL BITS

A sixty-minute documentary on Canadian peacekeeping could be searched to extract a three-minute section on peacekeeping in Egypt. The former might be too long to use in a classroom, while the latter would be ideal for classroom use, in a television documentary, or on a CD-ROM about Egypt.

Indexing News

What is the value of yesterday's news? Up until now, it hasn't been worth much. Old news is a contradiction in terms. Digital media, however, are breathing new life and value into old news and sports archives. There are many potential uses for these after they have been indexed and marked up.

A multimedia scrapbook would make a great birthday present if it contained newspaper, radio, and television news clips produced on the day you were born, or on one of your previous birthdays. Sports fans might want to reconstruct a favorite athlete's career as he or she played for different teams, with game highlights drawn from old broadcasts.

National network news programs are usually stored in vaults as videotapes with only the simplest of identifiers, usually the date of the broadcast. In that format they have almost no value. If you were interested in using the news to track the career of Lucien Bouchard, say, you would have to do a lot of research before you could pinpoint the dates he might have appeared on TV newscasts. You would have to get permission to view the likely newscasts, viewing hundreds of hours of material for perhaps a single item of use.

On the other hand, once news broadcasts are marked-up and indexed, you will be able to simply search for Lucien Bouchard, find the appropriate broadcast items, and then view just the relevant segments of the newscasts. Users would be willing to pay a reasonable price for such access, perhaps a low fee for browsing and higher fees for licensing a video segment for a specific use such as inclusion in a presentation, a television program, or a CD-ROM.

Indexing Video

The task of indexing the immense video archives that exist throughout the world is daunting. Applications have been developed to assist in the automation of such mark-ups, but in the end they all rely on knowledgeable and expensive experts who can recognize the context of the video and enter appropriate key words and descriptions for each section.

Thankfully, there are computer applications that simplify the process of indexing the video material. As the video is digitized, text indexes and mark-ups that describe the video are inserted into the digital video file along with a time-code locator. These insertions allow portions of the material to be easily searched and retrieved.

For new productions, the task of marking up video could be done at the production stage. This is when production personnel have the contextual data at hand, such as the names of actors in the footage and the intention of the filmmaker. Using appropriate software, an operator could add descriptive material on the fly while viewing the video. Current applications allow an operator to affix a time-code to the marked-up segment, so it may be quickly found. Indexing legacy (existing) videos will spawn a small industry of service bureaus that will specialize in providing indexing services to corporate and government clients.

Indexing Still Images

In some respects, still images present a more difficult mark-up problem than videos do. Photographs are frequently selected because of their color, graphical composition or style. So marking them up requires more careful thought and planning than just noting the subject matter and context.

BAGEL BITS

Searching a large image database using the word "cat" might yield hundreds or thousands of images, only a few of which might be appropriate to your need. You might need a picture of a cat for a cat food ad, for the logo of a pet shop, for an essay on wild cats, or for a documentary on Impressionist paintings of cats.

The Art Gallery of Ontario is part of AMICO, a consortium of North American galleries and museums making art collections available on-line. AMICO has made hundreds of thousands of images available to universities around the world. For an annual fee, students, faculty, and researchers can use the images, which are protected from digital theft, by technologies that weave the owner's identification invisibly into the digital data, and by finger-printing, which weaves the end user's identification invisibly into the digital data.

Indexing Audio

Audio content began its conversion to digital formats long before the other content types because of the advent of digital compact disc technology. Audio CDs provided an accepted standard technology for both new recordings and the conversion of legacy materials. So, although a large amount of old audio material has yet to be converted, virtually all audio recorded over the past decade is in digital formats. Much of this material has been marked up for sound-effect libraries and music CDs.

There is, however, a great deal of contextual information that cannot be stored within the digital audio CD standard. This includes liner notes, cover illustrations, and other related information.

There continues to be a commercial market for early music recordings and these are being digitized and sonically refurbished. After they are in digital format, older recordings are analyzed for audio faults such as tape hiss, record scratches, and low-frequency hum. Sophisticated digital processing equipment is able to find these faults and then to effectively subtract them from the recordings. The much-improved recordings are then transferred to CDs where they will last for many years without degrading, sounding better than they did when they were first recorded.

Indexing Text

Text indexing is the most highly developed digital markup technology. All current textbooks, reference books, magazines, and periodicals contain tables of contents and indexes that allow for searching on key words. These are available for digital databases since text has been prepared on computers, for at least the past decade.

Marked up text databases like the WestLaw legal precedents have demonstrated the value of these techniques. Such repositories of information generate significant income because interested parties can access portions of their content with relative ease.

Additional context is required, however, to make text more accessible. The number one request of database users is for summaries of articles and book chapters that greatly assist a researcher hone in what he or she is looking for. But manually constructing summaries is very time-consuming and requires expertise and for these reasons is often not commercially feasible. The good news is that computer programs are beginning to do this work quickly and inexpensively.

BAGEL BITS

The word processor that was used to write this book has an AutoSummarize function that does just that. Although it sometimes produces weird results, it is amazing how well it can extract meaningful content from each chapter and condense it to a fraction of its original size. Digital books and manuals will doubtless offer summaries at the head of each chapter in the near future.

Indexers

It is uncertain who will bear the high cost of indexing and marking up existing works. At one point the CBC was willing to license on-line rights to some of its programs for no fee provided the licensee indexed and marked up the programs in digital formats and gave the CBC rights to use the marked-up content.

By the turn of the century, broadband networks will be generally available throughout most of North America. These will be commerce-friendly (secure and administered), and will deliver a full range of multimedia content including illustrations, videos, audio, and marked-up text in a secure and managed environment. The consumer base will be sufficient to trigger meaningful revenue, which will accelerate the mark-up of networked data. In addition, as has been shown on the Internet, there are thousands of hobbyists and dabblers who will happily mark up information without fee, provided it's in their area of interest.

BAGEL BITS

Hundreds of thousands of music files are located throughout the Internet in the MIDI — Musical Instrument Digital Interface — format. These represent every type of pop and classical music. You can go to one of the archived music Web sites, search for a song by title, composer, or artist, and then hear it play on your computer.

Each of these song files was keyed in by a hobbyist musician who spent an average of four hours constructing the file. Some songs have lyrics and guitar chords entered as well as the musical notes. If this musical data were created commercially, the work would have cost hundreds of millions of dollars, and there would need to be a substantial fee for accessing the files. But the files are free because the work was done by people whose motivation was recreation and enjoyment.

Information from Governments

Statistics, up-to-date reports, and information are being made available to the public today that have in the past been accessible only to select groups within governments. This newly available information is being discussed and debated on the public networks, which is resulting in a more informed and powerful electorate.

I had a discussion with Canadian Heritage Minister Sheila Copps about the potential for citizens to vote electronically and directly on individual government agenda items. She argued that, while politicians have the staff, resources, and responsibility to investigate issues in detail, individual citizens tend to react emotionally to the quick headline or sound-bite or video-bite in the mass media. She implied that direct democracy would result in less informed decisions, influenced more by eloquent presenters than by the facts and contexts.

Today, however, we do have in-depth resources on the Internet that provide information, links to other information, and the widest range of opinons. From simple pork barrel politics to complex issues like nuclear power, politicians are being forced to put their positions forward with increasing detail and depth on the nets. The result is an increasingly informed citizenry.

Informing Government

E-mail allows users to send messages directly to their governments, flowing information to both elected representatives and public servants. Until recently, writing a letter to your councilor, mayor, member of provincial parliament, or the prime minister took some time and effort, as did circulating a petition by mail or door-to-door.

BAGEL BITS

Today's voters need only drag an e-mail address onto an e-note and it will reach their government representative within the hour. Adding the e-mail addresses of several representatives takes just additional seconds, but is the equivalent of sending many separate letters. Petitions have been known to gather hundreds of thousands of e-mail signatures within a few hours of circulation.

Retailers and Customers

Retailers have already had to change the way they do business in response to better-informed shoppers connected to comparative shopping data. Car buyers used to have a difficult time comparing quotes from different dealers because of the bewildering array of optional equipment and service plans that varied among dealers. Today shoppers can post their vehicle requirements on the Internet and wait for bids from many dealers, who have to respond to the customer's exact specifications or lose the sale. This is clearly putting the customer in the driver's seat, a Bagel Effect dividend.

In addition to text, sound, and video, simulations are playing a growing role in informing customers about products. Skiers are getting a virtual trip down the hill and into the après-ski lounge, and auto buffs are hearing the sound of a Ferrari's engine. Hardware chains will soon take your order on the Web and confirm they have stock of the hinge you need, before you make a wasted trip to your local store.

Direct shopper input will allow retailers to keep better control of inventories, and that should reduce prices. Ultimately, shoppers will be able to create demand for products that don't yet exist, and enterprising business people will react by manufacturing those products and making them available. The fundamental change will be from marketing *push* to demand *pull*, with shoppers gaining more control in the transaction. Shoppers will view retailers more as their agents and less as suppliers of a restricted line of products.

Person-to-Person

As more and more households get connected, people will communicate more frequently with each other. Word-of-mouth has always been an important means of passing on information, but in the past it has been restricted to physical meetings and then to telephone conversations. Networks allow individuals to become broadcasters, sending messages to a thousand people in a newsgroup as easily as to a single friend.

BAGEL BITS

When the Stonehaven West interactive community was first built, the new technologies and appliances were confusing to many families. Initially, 30% of the families did not own a computer. CulTech Research Centre and Bell Canada set up a twenty-four-hour help line and provided staff to answer residents' questions and solve problems. When the first residents moved in, we had help calls daily. We tutored, fixed, and generally informed the trial participants about their equipment and services. After about two months the calls stopped. Except for the occasional equipment malfunction, there have been no more calls for help.

What happened? It turns out that local kids took to the new technologies quickly; no surprise there. Because the community was wired, they were able to quickly and easily communicate with each other, with their families, and with their neighbors. They evolved into a community self-help support group.

This example demonstrates the power of interactive community information pools. The business case for digital services frequently hinges on the cost of ongoing service and maintenance. Since, in this case, the users were looking after it on their own, the prognosis for commercial viability improved.

20 ENTERTAINMENT
Culture or Business?

Entertainment has always been intricately entwined with culture and learning. Listening to music or watching television, activities we normally think of as entertaining, are important mechanisms for acquiring information and culture.

Some of the most effective learning is couched in entertaining contexts such as nursery rhymes (music, poetry), animations (visual arts), and plays (theater). The largest segment of the CD-ROM market is comprised of children's educational titles filled with entertaining games, music, animations, and role-playing simulations.

Mass Entertainment

Mass entertainment reaches mass markets via the mass media. Books, movies, computer games, and television programs continue to dominate our cultural landscape, putting universal plots in cultural wrappers that reflect our society. These entertainments also form the myths we carry through our lives. Teenagers are more likely to quote a moral lesson from an episode of *Beverly Hills 90210* than from a passage in the Bible.

In addition to providing us with popular culture, entertainment provides a great deal of incidental learning. When I was a little kid I loved comic books. My two favorites were *Uncle Scrooge* and *Classic Comics*. Between these two I gained a knowledge of Greek mythology (a specialty of Carl Barks, Scrooge's creator) and the world's great literature before I was ten years old. No one suspected I was learning anything including me. Years later when I regurgitated stories about the mythological Minotaur and *Wuthering Heights* to my teachers, they assumed I had a culturally rich childhood. Truth is, I did.

National Regulation

The Internet, a transnational network that knows no national boundaries, makes it difficult to impose national cultural regimes on producers or distributors. What is the point of requiring Canadian Web sites to treat Canadian content equally or preferentially to foreign content if the Web site operator can move to a server outside Canada and avoid regulation?

Imagine that Quebec secedes from Canada in order to maintain its local language and culture only to discover that these continue to be eroded by the English-language content and culture on the Internet. Even HTML, the underpinning language for the World Wide Web, is based on English.

User Regulation

As regulation moves from governments to individuals it will be up to each of us to determine whether we wish to block or accept content based on its cultural components — language, country of origin, region of origin, use of sexually explicit language and images, and so on.

User choice could work like this: Content providers would be asked to voluntarily fill out information fields that would be attached to content files. These fields could include suitability for children in certain age ranges, languages used, violence levels, sex levels, and so on. Users would then set filters on their browsers to only accept content for themselves or their children that meets certain requirements.

ᗷᗩᑕᗷᒪ ᗷITᔕ

A parent might set a filter for a child that only passes content suitable for children eight years old and under. Suppliers who filled out this field positively would have their content made available to the child. Suppliers who filled out the field negatively or not at all would have their content blocked. Parents who didn't set filters for their children would allow all content to be accessed.

Humor

Amid the thousands of special-interest groups (SIGs) on the Internet are Web sites devoted to humor, and these are among the most popular. They deserve special mention because, unlike most Internet sites, the sites themselves are not particularly interactive. There are jokes-of-the-day, comedian-branded Web sites, well-known and amateur comic-strips, collections of funny news stories, special-interest jokes (for computer geeks, politics aficionados, and so on), collections of funny excerpts from the public record (particularly from trials), and funny material generated by netizens who e-mail the stuff to their e-pals.

As aspect of this unique network culture of humor-consumers allows them to participate in this entertainment proactively. Upon receiving humorous material, most read it, decide which e-pals, if any, would likely get a chuckle out of it, and then forward it appropriately. If each user forwards a humorous document to an average of eight others, more than two million people will receive the jokes after only seven forwarding iterations.

Perhaps most significantly, humor-consumers most frequently edit the material and/or add their own comments before forwarding it. In this way, they gain some control over the entertainment. That's impossible in the normal media, and a nice example of the Bagel Effect.

Music

Chapter 13 deals with the music CD business in Canada, and as discussed there, the retailing of physical objects carrying digital intellectual property will flip into the new form of on-demand music services, and most of the retail music stores will close. Their business is already being eroded by record clubs (catalog) and television-direct sales.

In addition to on-line sales, retail outlets which cater to vertical niche markets such as jazz, blues, and dance will thrive, as will CD superstores that can afford to maintain a staff with expert knowledge about many areas of music.

Super-stores stock thousands of classical, jazz, and pop titles. Buyers shop at these locations not only for the variety of music, but also for the knowledgeable staff who can direct them to the CD they're searching for, or suggest one they might enjoy. The business of record stores in malls is being cannibalized by Internet sales of CDs, but well-stocked retail outlets with expert help are thriving.

This is true of future information delivery in general — there will be fewer outlets, but with more individualized and knowledgeable assistance to help find what you need. In digital network parlance, the outlets are called *portals* and the assistance is in the form of digital, not human, assistants. Generally the cost of setting up a digital sales outlet is greater than setting up a physical shop, but the costs of servicing clients are much lower on a network.

Film

Chapter 15 explains the fundamental changes taking place as film is being replaced by digital technologies. Home theaters that display digitized movies will drive a new movies-on-demand business and large theaters that exhibit production-heavy blockbuster movies will continue to thrive.

As the cost of delivering video programs on-demand to homes declines, so does the viability of neighborhood video stores. These retailers, many of whom add considerable value to the rental transaction with their staff's expert knowledge about movies, will have to either adapt to the new media — go into the business of digital retailing on networks — or go out of business.

Companies like Disney who have been able to sell millions of copies of their movies through video stores will have to retrench and get back into the business of ephemeral content — content that exists only for a brief period of time while it is being consumed. That's not to say that kids and adults won't want physical goods that relate to movies — posters, fluffy toys, and so on — but they won't want or need to own the videotapes.

Television

Television will move substantially to user-controlled programming models with programs-on-demand offering viewers choice and the ability to match scheduling to their availability. Broadcast-type channels will continue for real-time events like news and sports because they have an immediacy the audience wants.

The entire television industry will change, not just because digital TVs will lead to convergence with computers and digital networks, but because new appliances will receive television signals in new audience environments.

As television signals become available on computer screens in offices and on flat-screen monitors in kitchens, the content will have to change. The huge gap that exists today between computer applications and television programs will blur and soon vanish. Cooking programs on television today will have new utility as video resources coupled with recipe programs that will compute the necessary ingredients for your evening dinner. And business television programs will have adjunct applications to track your personal investments and place buy-and-sell orders as up-to-the-minute financial information flits across your television screen.

Indies Gaining Ground

The success of independent film, record, and television producers is breaking the majors' control over the production. At the 1997 Academy Awards in Hollywood, 163 films vied for recognition as the best in the world. Only one of the nominated pictures was produced by a major Hollywood studio. The rest were independent productions that had much greater freedom to break out of the Hollywood story and packaging formulas. It was an important indication of the Bagel Effect at work, as freedom and control moved to the edges of the moviemaking system.

Games

Arcade and video games are primarily entertainment. However, when we play a game, we are learning and practicing strategic thinking, problem-solving, hand-eye coordination, and other skills. Video games empower kids. What other activity can a young person get involved in where they can control their environment and have a fair chance at triumphing over adversity?

Far from being a waste of valuable school time, gaming will enter the school system and influence traditional course materials. Nintendo, SONY, and Sega may finally wake up to the potential of games as education. If they don't, they will be eclipsed by new companies that get it.

Culture or Just Fun

There remains a great controversy about whether entertainment products are fundamentally industrial or cultural in nature. The United States, which controls the bulk of the world's entertainment products, refuses to acknowledge their cultural impact, because doing so would exempt these products from free-trade legislation and allow countries to regulate their importation and sale. Canada, like most European countries, refers to book and magazine publishing, music, cinema, theater, and television as cultural industries while the United States calls them entertainment industries.

The difference is very significant from the standpoint of national and cultural integrity but also from the standpoint of business. Canadian government support for local culture/entertainment has had major impacts on the careers of artists ranging from Anne Murray and Bryan Adams to Margaret Atwood and Atom Egoyan. They have benefited from regulated Canadian content rules for broadcasters, postal subsidies for Canadian books and magazines, and government arts council grants.

Under free-trade agreements, Canada's trading partners view these forms of support as biased unfairly against foreign entertainment business interests. Within most countries, however, these supports are seen as preservations of national culture and identity. The issue is a hot topic, not only in Canada but also throughout the world, especially in Europe. There, countries are fighting fiercely to maintain their national language and customs in the wake of the powerful Hollywood distribution system that brings American language and culture into everyone's bedrooms, livingrooms, and Internet browsers.

Distribution Monopolies

The Bagel Effect suggests that large multinational distribution companies, *the majors*, will lose absolute control of the industry as it moves from capital-intensive physical networks of manufacturing plants, trucks, trains, planes, and warehouses to digital networks in which the financial barriers to entry are low.

A mere half-dozen companies in the world control the distribution of more than three-quarters of all movies and music. They are multinational and transnational in scope. SONY is Japanese, EMI is British, BMG is German, Warner Brothers is American, MCA/Universal and Polygram are Canadian, purchased by Edgar Bronfman Jr. in the late '90s. Nonetheless, most of the content the majors create, along with the content created for television, is produced in Hollywood, California. Hollywood remains the entertainment capital of the world.

So, although the government of Canada may not be able to prevent American exhibitors from controlling Canadian cinema screens, the technology of Internet-like networks will allow many more producers of entertainment content access to the same Canadian eyeballs and ears. Large companies will continue to have commercial advantages, such as access to capital and human resources for promoting and marketing their products. The difference is that they will no longer be able to exclude others from distributing their products to audiences.

BAGEL BITS

The constitutional right to bear arms and the glorification of violence and villains are key themes in American culture. From the outset, American films have featured cowboys and Indians killing each other, and have romanticized gangsters like Jesse James, Bonnie and Clyde, and Mafioso. Science fiction movies like **Star Wars** have generally substituted white and black space suits for white and black cowboy hats, projecting armed conflicts into the future and outside our solar system.

European and Canadian films do not generally share this obsession with violence. However, the American cultural bias will continue to prevail so long as they maintain their dominance over the world's entertainment production.

The advent of Bagel Effects with its attendant localization poses a great threat to Hollywood's control of the distribution channels for entertainment. They will not give up that control easily.

21 CULTURE AND THE ARTS
Public or Private Funding

The arts' primary function is to mirror humanity, not produce a commercial result. Government funding for the arts had risen significantly for about forty years, but has recently gone into decline. The new model encourages increased private sector funding, and fits with the Bagel Effect.

Public Art Is Not New

The expression of culture through works of art is evident in every society. As 50,000-year-old cave paintings in the south of France illustrate, art was very important to people in prehistoric times. Even back then, the community supported the creation of art.

The complexity of the paintings and artifacts found in excavations and caves demonstrates that artists spent a great deal of time on their work. The time and effort necessary to invent and make materials such as paints and brushes — technologies — suggest that artists could not have participated in their share of tribal hunting and gathering. They must have been given sustenance by their clan so they could express their culture.

Throughout history, rulers have patronized the arts for their personal edification and to propagate the cultures they represented. This was as true of the Medici family in Renaissance Italy as it was of the Communists in the twentieth century. Even the artifacts and hieroglyphics of ancient Egypt attest to the importance of the arts and culture to the government of the time.

In feudal times artworks illustrated the faces, lifestyles, and ideologies of the ruling class. As governments moved from feudal to democratic forms, arts patronage moved from royalty to taxpayers with the result that the cultures of Europe and North America are now depicted in artworks with the faces, lifestyles, and ideologies of ordinary people.

Twentieth Century Support for Arts

In the middle of the twentieth century, central governments began taking a larger role in supporting the arts. Municipal, state, and provincial arts councils were set up, as was the National Endowment of the Arts in the United States and the Canada Council. But as we near the turn of the century these organizations are being jeopardized by funding cuts, which reflect popular thinking that the arts should be supported by private patrons and paying audiences and that government should get out of the area of cultural subsidies.

This Bagel Effect suggests that the decentralization of arts support will continue for at least the next decade.

The Age of Philanthropy

With the rise of democracy and capitalism came an age of philanthropy in which many of the great private foundations were set up in the United States. The Carnegies, the Fords, and others were motivated to give large gifts to the arts by a sense of public spirit and a belief in democratic access to culture. By the middle of the twentieth century, however, the growth of government had fostered a legislated social consciousness with tax laws that encouraged charitable giving, offering generous tax breaks to arts supporters.

Much of what appears to be private giving is in fact public giving. Unlike the philanthropists who gave their own money to the arts in the nineteenth century, twentieth century patrons receive large tax breaks for supporting the arts. Since the tax system is deprived of this revenue, the rest of the tax-payers end up footing the bill.

Henry R. (Hal) Jackman, a great Canadian arts patron and current Chair of the Ontario Arts Council, said in a speech to the press in early 1997, "the establishment of tax incentives and Crown Foundations encourages patrons to give gener-ously because they can direct their gifts ... but it's still mostly public money." In this way, private giving has become just another form of public giving. But as the public continues to foot the bill, it is deprived of the public accountability that comes with government programs. A cynic might suggest that the rich get to play while the rest have to pay.

Whether governments, individuals, or corporations directly support the arts, the money still comes primarily from all tax-payers, so public access and administration of the arts are important. Those that pay should have a say.

Biting the Bagel

The weaning of governments from the administration of grants to the arts is in keeping with the Bagel Effect of decen-tralization and decreasing government intervention.

Personal Experience

When I began my term as chairman of the board of the Ontario Arts Council in 1995, the Council's budget was $43 million. OAC was the largest regional supporter of the arts in all of North America. I had been using knowledge of the Bagel Effect to help industries restructure their business, and I applied the same principles for structural changes at the Arts Council. I hoped these would better position OAC to weather the financial storms to come.

The storms did come! Within two years, the OAC budget had been slashed to $26 million, a decrease of 40%. Although the pain of decreased funding was acute within the arts community and at the Arts Council, the changes that were made allowed OAC to survive and emerge as a new-style organization, attuned to the realities of a community seeking lower public spending and fewer public programs. Here's what we did.

The Bagel Effect suggests smaller administration, and so OAC cut its staff dramatically, by about half. Internal operations were contracted out, when it was more economical to do so. Many in-house staff were reorganized into teams that were allocated to the departments of dance, music, theater, literature, and media arts as they were needed — just-in-time deployment. Application forms were redesigned to make it easier to apply for assistance. We blended our databases with the municipal councils — Toronto Arts Council and Metro Toronto Arts Council — which cut red tape for projects funded by several levels of government. OAC developed up-to-date arts management computer software and then licensed it to other organizations like the Canada Council.

In addition to delivering grants, OAC added many client-oriented services, such as research and advocacy assistance. Local communities could count on OAC to help them with local initiatives. OAC created new staff positions and new budget items to accommodate client-initiated projects that didn't fit existing programs. The entire corporate culture was skewed towards client service instead of institutional programs. The clients were everyone we dealt with — artists, arts organizations, and the communities they serve. Like industry and government, the new catchphrase became "What can we do to help you?"

The Canada Council also began implementing policies that recognized the Bagel Effect realities. In addition to cutting its administration, it established a new endowment, funded by artists who achieved commercial success after receiving public support in the early stages of their careers.

Encouraging Private Donors

A Foundation for the Arts in Ontario was created to encourage and accept private gifts. This new OAC Foundation administers private funds according to the wishes of individual donors. The OAC Foundation has already accumulated more than $20 million in endowment funds and these will continue to grow every year, generating an increasingly significant portion of support to artists and cultural organizations.

While I concentrated on organizational changes at OAC, I missed a brewing board-level problem that blew up in the second year of my term. The Chalmers family had been OAC's greatest private patron. Over the years, they had given more than $10 million of their money for distribution by OAC to artists. Joan Chalmers had been monitoring the increased control being given to private arts donors, and bristled at the terms of her family's gifts to OAC — they specified that her family would have *no* control over the utilization of the funds. She asked that her father's Trust Agreement be set aside and that some control over the funds be given back to the family. We couldn't accommodate her because her father was no longer alive to change the agreement. Frustrated at what she perceived as our intransigence, she lashed out publicly at the OAC for being unresponsive to private donors.

In retrospect, OAC should have been more responsive to Joan's concerns, although the legal aspects of our position dictated that we respond publicly as we did. After almost a year of conversations, negotiations, and good will on both sides, we did find a solution that satisfied both the Chalmers and OAC's lawyers. The root of the issue was a clear Bagel Effect — moving power and control away from the center of an organization, in this case the OAC. I regret that I didn't spot this before it exploded. I'm certain the brew-ha-ha could have been circumvented.

A Trillion Dollars Will Change Hands

More than $1 trillion will change hands in Canada over the next twenty years as many of our aging population reach their four-score years. There is an excellent opportunity for arts and cultural organizations to tap into these funds that will become available over the coming decades. It is fertile ground to solicit a fraction of these as bequests; especially from elderly people who may not have close living relatives to pass their wealth to. If used as endowment funds, these monies could provide ongoing support for the arts without being subject to the quicksilver verisimilitudes of government budgeting.

By reaching out to private giving generally directed by donors to specific activities, we are in line with the Bagel megatrend that puts more control in the hands of individuals.

Art on the Web

The World Wide Web is a most effective tool for marketing and promoting arts. Monika Lugas, a painter and sculptor from Cobourg, Ontario, has catalogs of her works available on the Web. In addition, she maintains a biography, list of public exhibitions, and personal information about herself. Her husband, Rod Anderson, is a poet, lyricist, and composer who makes his works available directly from their Web site, performing the roles of author, publisher, promoter and vendor — all from his home.

BAGEL BITS

The Canadian Music Centre, an Ontario Arts Council client, promotes the use of Canadian music and maintains a database of music scores, parts, and recordings. In the first six weeks they went on-line with a Web site they had more clients access their music than had in the previous six months at all their offices across the country.

Networked Digital Distribution

The advent of networked digital distribution may offer an alternate distribution route for cultural products, an option that could have many beneficial side effects. The elimination of manufacturing and warehousing means that many more producers of artworks can make them available virtually and market them directly, bypassing the large distributors who have shown no interest in marketing works without mass appeal.

This could be to the great advantage of artists whose works are not in the popular mainstream and for consumers with more eclectic tastes. Since consumers and creators are the big winners here, this change is very Bagel-friendly.

Co-Mingling Arts and Entertainment

Your physical environment has an important effect on whether you perceive something as art or entertainment. When you go to a cinema, your frame of mind is entertainment, but when you watch a film or video in an art gallery, you bring a greater esthetic sensibility to your viewing. When artworks are presented on digital media alongside entertainment products, the context differentiation dissolves.

The McLuhan suggestion that *messages are modified by media* applies particularly to digital media, which tends to vulgarize art and elevate entertainment by co-mingling them side-by-side in the same exhibition environment. In general, artists have the most to gain, because their works will be available to audiences who would not generally go to a concert-hall or art gallery.

BAGEL BITS

It may not be possible to implement Canadian content regulations on digital networks because, unlike broadcasting, the supplier cannot control the content selection. However, it is certainly possible to encourage the availability of Canadian creations on digital networks. There are software applications that could ensure that Canadian content gets a fair share of the users' attention.

One idea would give preferential shelf space, so to speak, to Canadian content. You ask for the news and you are presented with a list of twenty news services ranging from Associated Press to CNN. It is possible to ensure that the top three options, say, would be Canadian services.

Similarly, music, movies, television programs, and text files could be flagged as Canadian and treated by browsers, search engines, and Web sites in a manner that would ensure that Canadians get a fair share of eyeballs and ears on the net.

22 INTELLECTUAL PROPERTY
Will Creators Gain Control of their Works

Intellectual property consists of original works that exist outside of their physical expression. Shakespeare's *Julius Caesar*, may be printed as a book, John Lennon's *Imagine* may be pressed as a CD, Picasso's *Guernica* may be painted on canvas, Microsoft's *Windows* operating system may be duplicated on floppy disks, and the anti-depressant "Prozak" may be manufactured as a pill, but these physical manifestations are just particular expressions of the underlying creations. Nonetheless, the law only protects physical manifestations of intellectual property. You can't copyright an idea, only a play, novel, or song that is expressed as a performance, a book or a CD.

This situation poses a problem when intellectual property is expressed digitally on a network because the physical property is not so clear — bits of data. The problem is exacerbated because intellectual properties are precisely the ones that are most easily distributed digitally, and among the most valuable. Intellectual property has become one of the most important and contentious concepts in the digital age.

Intellectual property — IP — is defined and protected by copyright, patent, and trademark legislation throughout the world. Although laws protecting intellectual property go back a few hundred years, the concept of creator rights pre-dates history. Many aboriginal groups hold that a song is the property of its composer, and no one else in the tribe may sing it. The same is frequently true of artworks, such as totem poles, whose underlying stories are considered the property of a tribe, closely guarded from outsiders.

Physical Versus Intellectual Property

If I own a piece of physical property, I can sell it. If it's a car, for instance, its total value is the selling price. I sell the car, get the money, and no longer own the car. If I create a piece of intellectual property (IP), I can license it. If it's a song, for instance, its value exceeds the payments for its expression on a CD. I license the song, get paid royalties, but I still own the song. I can license it again and again for inclusion in other CDs and, if it becomes a hit, its value will increase substantially.

Since the twenty-first century will bring a content-driven economy, it's important that IP be carefully managed. But the digital revolution and convergence create problems for managing IP. The problems relate to laws and business practices that were formulated for creations expressed as objects, not digits.

Bagels and IP

Intellectual property presents a challenge for Bagel Effect analysis. We expect the creators and consumers (at the edges of the production/distribution system) will benefit at the expense of producers and distributors. But creators and users have opposed each other when it comes to intellectual property rights. For example, consumer groups lobby against patent protection for medicines, against the interests of inventors. Similarly, netizens demand free content on the Internet, against the interests of writers, composers, visual artists, and computer programmers.

BAGEL BIT

The latter decades of the twentieth century have seen a much greater concentration of power and control in a few global intellectual property companies that control the newspaper, broadcasting, film, and record industries. They have been wresting control of copyrights and patents from individual creators, a decidedly creampuff activity. Will authors and their kin regain control of their creations at the start of the millennium, or will intellectual property become an anomaly of the Bagel Effect?

This is a great test for the Bagel Effect, one whose outcome will help determine the haves and the have-nots in the twenty-first century's new order.

Intellectual Property Food Chain

The traditional chain of delivering IP to an end user works like this.

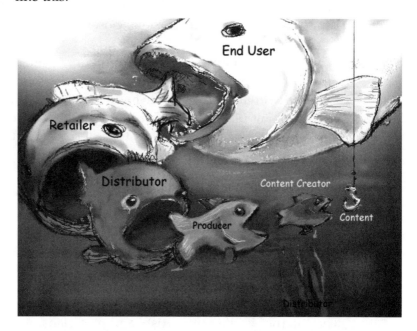

Figure 22.1 — Intellecutal Property Food Chain

The creator is the original content owner and has the initial rights to the IP. The rights of individual creators are bundled together by a producer who packages IP into a product for commercial exploitation. On digital networks, the producer is sometimes associated with the Web site creator. A distributor is licensed by the producer to promote and sell the product to retailers who, in turn, promote and sell the product to users. In the parlance of an IP food chain, the user consumes the product.

In the case of digital online distribution, the IP chain may be collapsed. When books, magazines, music, movies, computer programs, and other content are delivered digitally, there is no need for manufacturing plants, warehouses, and transportation by trucks, trains, and planes. This means that the traditional roles of distributor and retailer may be collapsed into a single promotion and sales entity — the online store. In keeping with the Bagel Effect, it eliminates bureaucratic and administrative levels and brings the user closer to the supplier.

A massive shift in business practice occurs when a creator or producer sells products directly to consumers eliminating both of the sales organizations in the middle of the food chain. This shift is taking place for content that has not warranted mass marketing and distribution. This type of content is beginning to find distribution directly by owners to consumers.

The World Wide Web abounds with examples of direct creator-to-consumer sites. Whether it's a cartoonist placing his strips on-line because he doesn't have a syndication deal or a poet whose works do not have a sufficiently wide audience to support publication in a book, netizens are being exposed to a wide range of works that come directly from their creators.

The Internet is rife with artists and musicians offering their works for sale. They can do so without the cost and intervention of professional aggregators, distributors, or retailers. The creators have to promote their own works, but this is feasible with online distribution. The Bagel Effect is evident since the customer gets to negotiate directly with the creator, leaving the transaction entirely at the edges of the system with no central intervention.

Intellectual Property Management

The management of intellectual property includes protecting it from theft and piracy and accounting for its use so owners can be paid. Such systems need to balance the needs of consumers, who want easily accessible and inexpensive content, with the needs of suppliers, who want payment, security, and control of their properties in the new media.

Once content is in digital formats and marked up for use, it needs to be enrolled in databases, which will record the names of the owners, the terms for usage, and so on. Unique international identifiers will travel with each work so that appropriate credits and payments can be made regardless of where the work was consumed.

In March 1996, at the Technology Based Intellectual Property Management symposium sponsored by the Copyright Office and the International Multimedia Association in Washington, D.C., my colleagues and I presented a specification for such a content management system: IVY.

IVY is a comprehensive framework for networked commerce. It enables secure authorized and authenticated transactions among consumers, retailers, and distributors. Users can receive data, services, or other content ephemerally (in real-time) or by downloading (printing, copying to a disk). IVY relies on contract law and technology as its underpinnings, with copyright and patent laws as strengthening agents.

IVY enrolls content items (identifies, encrypts, and links to agreements specifying terms and conditions of use), it authorizes and authenticates distributors and consumers who have permission to access the content, and it accounts for all accesses on digital networks. Together the IVY functions give content owners the assurance that they will get fair accounting and payment for their works and services.

IVY has been used on the Intercom Ontario digital network since December 1996. It has been accounting for actions, interactions, and transactions including the use of music-on-demand, CD-ROMs on-demand, educational courses, health care, and Internet use.

Copyrights and E-Rights

Rights to intellectual property originally in print are a hot topic these days, but there is no consensus on how they may be dealt with in law or practice. The electronic rights (e-rights) are important because, if companies can turn a profit in the new media, they will spend money to build up the new infrastructure. If not, and that's been the case so far, the Infoway will remain a country road with few on-ramps for some time to come. The Bagel Effect argues that creators will regain control of their works.

In fact, journalists have been taking their publishers to court claiming that they never relinquished the digital distribution rights to their articles when they wrote them for print publication. Writers are particularly miffed that publishers have been earning income from distributing their works digitally without paying them a portion of the proceeds.

Publishing agreements have traditionally included catch-all clauses for new rights. They usually read something like "... creator assigns all rights in all media now known or that may become available in the future." But the 1997 revision to Canada's Copyright Act, section 58.1, gives the new digital rights back to creators. It states "No agreement concluded before April 25, 1996 that assigns a right ... under this Act shall be construed as assigning or granting any rights conferred for the first time by this Act [digital rights] ..."

ᏴᎯᏩᎬᏞ ᏴᎥᏣᎦ

Canada's Copyright Board began hearing arguments for liability on the Internet in 1998. Its ruling on whether Internet access providers or Web site operators (or both) have to pay copyright holders for putting their content online will likely be appealed to the Supreme Court because the ramifications are so broad.

WIPO Treaties

On December 20, 1996, the World Intellectual Property Organization — WIPO — adopted the Performances and Phonograms Treaties. These recognize for the first time the rights of creators, performers, and producers in works distributed on new digital media. The treaties require that countries around the world enact national legislation to bring their laws into sync with the WIPO treaties. The result will be new distribution of movies, television programs, and music on digital networks, since stakeholders will have the legal rights they need to get paid for their content.

Without copyright legislation, we might continue with the current situation, in which most of the valuable music, books, and movies are not available on digital networks because owners don't want to give them away without assurance they will be fairly paid. Once liability for payment is established, the doors will be open for delivering full-fidelity music and high quality movies on new media.

Superdistribution

Many believe that the future of digital commerce and rights management lies in superdistribution, a system that vests the greatest choice and power with users. The term *super* in superdistribution has a meaning similar to its use in the word *super*conductivity — without resistance. In a superdistribution environment, digital content is made available freely yet is protected from unauthorized use. This is accomplished by encasing the content in the equivalent of display cases.

Users can view the encased contents if they abide by the terms of admission, but the content is protected from thieves and vandals. This is accomplished in cyberspace using digital encryptions that require authorizations and passwords for decoding, watermarking, and fingerprinting (see Chapter 19, Information). Whenever content is used in a superdistribution environment it *phones home* and notifies the owner about who used the content and how it was used.

Because only authorized users can access the content after they've complied with the terms and conditions for use, piracy is eliminated. Superdistribution allows the unrestricted copying and distribution of digital content. Although the content can't tell if it has been copied, it will record if it has been used.

For instance, if songs were made available digitally in superdistribution-type containers, you could freely download them or stream them over a network. You could make copies of the song, burn it onto a CD, or pass it to your friend. Each time you or your friend wanted to listen to the song, however, it would check to see that the environment in which you want to play it is within its terms and conditions for use. If so, you could listen to it, but it would send a message to a designated file server announcing its use and your name.

BAGEL BITS

The Bagel Effect predicts that superdistribution will flourish because it promotes freedom of use among individuals and takes control away from central management systems.

PART 6
YOUR PERSONAL BAGEL

The Lifelong Approach

During an exam, one of Albert Einstein's students is said to have whispered to the professor, "Dr. Einstein, the questions on this year's exam are exactly the same as the ones on last year's exam." Einstein paused for a moment and replied, "That may be so, but this year the answers are different."

The societies we live in impose structures on our lives. We are given to understand that the best structure is an initial period of institutional learning that prepares us for earning a living and raising a family, and that the final period will be retirement in leisure.

The Bagel Effect suggests that there will be major changes to the way we learn, the way we earn, the way we live in communities, and the way we take our leisure. These will be driven be greater individual freedoms and a reduced security net.

Life Has Changed

The division of life into three phases of learning, earning, and leisure is no longer appropriate because the world has shifted around us. The social, economic, and political structures that have fashioned the twentieth century three-phase life model have themselves gone out of fashion.

Life is different than it was fifty years ago. Young people no longer expect that they will be better off than their parents were. They no longer take for granted that they will enter an expanding work force when they complete a course of study at a trade school or university. They go to school longer, marry later, and generally both spouses work.

Birth control, a gender-neutral workplace, the explosion of information, and trends contributing to the Bagel Effect have changed our society in fundamental ways. Consequently, the answers to questions about how we should structure our lives are different now.

Lifelong Learning

Schooling now lasts well into a young person's twenties, and many professionals are entering the work force well into their thirties. We should be entering the work force much earlier. Teenagers have the energy and drive to be productive and they have been frustrated by their inability to do so. In the future, people will be entering the work force much earlier.

Although our formative schooling will be shorter, we will need to continue our education throughout our lives. There's just too much to learn to confine it to childhood and young adulthood. Lifelong learning is more necessary today because the things we need to know when we're thirty were probably not known when we were twenty.

Lifelong Earning

The need to finance lifelong learning coupled with diminishing government commitments to pension and health plans will require more contributions from individuals for their retirement.

In the corporate sector, downsizing and contracting-out work have caused massive disruptions in employee pension plans. People are changing jobs with increasing frequency and in many cases their pension benefits are lost with the job switch. The result is a widening gap between the cost of a worry-free retirement and the financial resources available. In order to close that financial gap we will have to work longer — start younger and end older.

Lifelong Leisure

The guaranteed retirement pension plans that governments provide are running out of money and the benefits will likely decrease over time. Since we'll be working longer it will be necessary to the way we take our leisure throughout our working years.

BAGEL BITS

Instead of three approximately equal life stages of learning, earning, and leisure, it will be more reasonable to take a less structured journey. The routes will be more tailored to each individual, according to our capabilities, our personalities, and our health. There will be fewer guarantees, fewer governmental supports, fewer job supports, greater risks, and a need for individuals to take charge of their own affairs.

If this sounds like the Bagel Effect, it's no coincidence. Just as the Bagel Effect suggests that organizations are becoming more fluid and less structured in the way they must operate, it brings the same conclusions to our personal lives.

23 LEARNING
What You Want, When You Want It

"Thirty years from now the big university campuses will be relics.... the cost of higher education has risen as fast as the cost of health care ... Such totally uncontrollable expenditures, without any visible improvement in either the content or the quality of education, means that the system is rapidly becoming untenable... Already we are beginning to deliver more lectures and classes off campus via satellite or two-way video at a fraction of the cost."

— "Universities Won't Survive", *Forbes Magazine*, March 1997.

Knowledge Is Power!

Knowledge is extremely valuable. Hunters who know animal habits are more likely to find prey and make a kill. Gatherers who know where to find edible plant foods are more productive and more likely to survive. Farmers who know when to plant and harvest crops are rewarded with higher yields. And stockbrokers who understand how corporations operate can make money for themselves and their clients.

Knowledge conveys power. As learning and training become more available through new media, they will bring new knowledge and power to those who access them. The groups that will access the new knowledge opportunities will not be limited to young people. They will include part-time and full-time students of all ages. They will include those who have changed jobs within their company or are at a new company. They will include entrepreneurs who need a quick study to enter a new market and people who want to learn for the pleasure of it.

Education will not be limited to institutional settings or set times. Insomniacs will want to learn at 4:00 a.m. Women who notice a lump in their breast and men who notice blood in their urine will want to learn about cancer symptoms, immediately. Parents whose four-year-olds teach themselves to read will want to learn about schooling for gifted children.

The educational framework was designed around the segmentation of our lives into fixed periods of formal education, productivity, and retirement. In the past, workers stayed with one or two employers throughout their productive years. A university graduate was pretty well assured of a job. The same was true for someone with a certificate from a recognized trade school. These expectations from the educational infrastructure are no longer valid because the job market has been turned inside out and because learning and training have become necessary long after formal schooling is over. As a result the current system is both too expensive and not responsive enough to social and industrial needs.

Our educational systems have taken longer to succumb to the Bagel Effect because they are heavily unionized and because their administrators are less capable of mandating structural change than those of other businesses. Changes in the public school system involve governments, local school boards, principals, staff, and parents. Students have had no say in their education until now but will be gaining control of it, according to Bagel predictions.

The time is ripe for change. The North American school system has been spurred to action by the budget cuts of the late '90s and is being dragged (kicking and screaming in most cases) into the same sorts of systemic re-engineering that have become common in other sectors.

Education Is Big Business

Education and training are big businesses. The billions we spend on learning is a big chunk of our economy, so any shift in the way education and training are delivered will have an enormous economic impact. These shifts have already started and we are beginning to see the massive effects that flow from them.

Up until now, the cost of primary and secondary school education has been funded publicly. The cost of community colleges, universities, and libraries has been funded by a combination of public funding and user fees while corporations have largely funded training. That's about to change.

The 1998 Lehman Brothers' *Investment Report on Education* forecasts that the educational market will eventually become dominated by EMO's — Education Maintenance Organizations — just as HMOs — Health Maintenance Organizations — have dominated the American healthcare market. The report states, "the (learning) business is potentially worth several hundred billion dollars. Investment opportunity in the education industry has never been better." Although this prognosis is aimed primarily at the United States, several Canadian provinces have begun to move in this direction by placing new course developments out to tender in the private sector.

A History of Creampuffs

Our universities echo the fortress mentalities of the Middle Ages, when their predecessors were established. Faculty tenure was originally brought to universities to ensure freedom of expression, but it has been used as a tool by twentieth century faculty unions to enshrine job security. In primary and secondary schools, teachers' unions and boards of education are both strongly opposed to structural changes because it means some of their members will lose their jobs.

The result is that the interests of school administrators and staff have come to override the interests of students. In Bagel parlance, these creampuff systems are laden with central controls and powerful suppliers who are reluctant to give up control over their clients.

Some countries are more hidebound in their educational systems than Canada and the United States. The French minister of education, while touring Canada, prided himself in looking at his watch from time to time and saying "At this moment every French grade-four student is learning geography." The pride was based on a system that supposedly guarantees a uniform education to every child.

The Bagel Effect suggests that every child should have access to an appropriate education, not necessarily the same one as every other child. It is time to recognize the strength in our diverse individual interests and abilities. The commonality of our learning systems should be in providing core competencies such as the ability to use information infrastructures to acquire new knowledge.

Focus on Students

Our educational systems are not responsive to students' needs. The reality today is that a post-secondary education no longer guarantees a job. People entering the work force expect to work at six or seven different jobs during their employable years as opposed to one or two jobs in the past. Even if you stay with the same employer for a long time you will need new training and skills to handle changes in your job description.

The situation has frustrated both students and employers. For those already on set career paths, the prospects are frightening. In a recent survey, more than three-quarters of surveyed workers said that, "no matter what I plan for the future, when I get there, it's always different." For employers, it's frustrating to see positions unfilled within their firm when so many workers are out of a job.

The new educational systems must deliver just-in-time learning so that skills and knowledge can be acquired as needed. This is in direct contrast to current systems that most frequently provide education that may be completely irrelevant while ignoring social and industrial needs.

For example, many students study calculus in high school because it is a prerequisite for taking university science courses. But for some science students, calculus is never required. It makes more sense to ensure that most high school students are exposed to the principles of science (including calculus) but that the complete sets of skills are not taught until they are required. This fits with a return to a broader, more general education in primary and secondary schools.

Governments Cuts to Education

Beginning with former U.S. President Ronald Reagan's reducing the funding for student loans and bursaries in the '80s, central governments have been reducing their financial support for education in an effort to cap costs and ultimately to reduce taxes.

In Canada, federal and provincial support for education has been steadily declining for half a decade. In order to make ends meet, universities and colleges have been raising student fees. Tuition, formerly capped by the government, is being deregulated, and in many cases has increased by 300% or more.

As tuitions rise, students are becoming more discriminating about where they buy their education and what they get for their money. This new consumer-styled attitude is putting additional stress on institutions that in the past have always attracted a full complement of students because tuition was so affordable. The new student-as-consumer is beginning to compare value from a larger number of education suppliers, both the traditional ones and those based on the new media. Schools will have to compete much more aggressively than in the past and institutions that won't make the transition to a market-sensitive approach will wither and close.

Cuts in primary and secondary schools are following suit. Alberta led the Canadian provinces in cutting its education infrastructure by eliminating many of its school boards and cutting funding drastically. Other provinces are moving in the same direction. On May 1, 1998, the *Toronto Star* proclaimed, "The Toronto District School Board plans to eliminate half of its middle managers, slashing 1,000 jobs over the next two years."

Private Schools

Governments are moving towards privatization of education. Private schools will increase in number and prosper as governments allow them to offer certification and degrees. The result will be a much less uniform educational system, more tailored to the individual needs and capabilities of students. This is in keeping with the Bagel Effect — moving towards individual control and away from central institutional control.

Private schools also offer students more course variety, bringing greater opportunities for teachers who have qualifications outside the core public school curricula. These teachers of art, music, drama, and other courses considered frills today will have a better chance for a job. Private schools tend to differentiate themselves to serve niche markets. Some are known for helping students who are having a tough time qualifying for university, some are focused on the arts, and some stress military-style discipline.

BAGEL BITS

There are a growing number of parents who place their children in private schools because they are above or below the average capabilities of their classmates. The public education system has forced students to conform to institutional needs and this has led to large heterogeneous classes in which slow students are left behind and bright students lose interest because they're bored. The new paradigm dictates catering to individual student needs.

Control Shifting to Students

The clear message is that we must shift the focus from teachers and institutions to learners and personalized courses of study. The phrase-of-the-day acknowledges that a teacher must change from a "sage on the stage" to a "guide on the side." This change in emphasis is consistent with the Bagel Effect. In the new paradigm, students will take a much more active part in their own learning.

Some changes have already taken place. In 1997, New York University began offering a masters degree delivered completely over the Internet. Students have the freedom of living anywhere in the world and the university does not have to provide physical facilities on campus. Both save money. Queens University has a Masters in Business Administration program available as distance learning for a tuition fee of $20,000. It's very popular among executives who want the course but can't move to Kingston to take it.

Several Canadian universities have formed a consortium called Virtual U, headquartered at Simon Fraser University in British Columbia, which is producing courseware for networked learning materials. York University is using CulTech's VITAL — Varied and Integrated Teaching and

Learning — system for delivering courses off campus, and Athabaska University is the first Canadian school to go entirely virtual — it does not have a campus at all. These are but a few examples of what is becoming an avalanche of new educational offerings by public and private educators.

Convergence in Education

The separate systems of universities, colleges, job training programs, and correspondence schools will converge along the lines of the new digital distribution channels so that students can have better access to all sorts of learning without geographic bias. As courseware and libraries become digitally linked throughout the world, students will have greater control over the materials they use and that will result in less power for institutional bureaucrats.

Institutions will be forced to differentiate their educational products by factors other than location since interactive courses are becoming globally available on networks. If you can take an interactive online engineering course from MIT, you might not pay as much for the same course given by an institution less highly rated in that field.

Learning Materials

The market for textbooks and learning materials will expand greatly. Today, textbooks are the primary teaching materials, but selection has been restricted to titles authorized by school boards and professors. Many more titles will become available to students and schools as the systems become less rigidly regulated. The greater variety of books and materials may result in lower sales volumes for individual titles. In marketing parlance this means broader and thinner penetration, a Bagel Effect.

CD-ROMs and other new media will take an increasing share of the market because they are interactive and tailored to the individual capability and learning pace of the student. CD-ROMs already form the major learning material for preschool children with the result that many kids are entering kindergarten and grade one with excellent reading and math skills.

In Canada, the federal SchoolNet program will have every public school in the country connected to the Internet by the year 2000. This is driving a new demand for curricula and course materials tailored to delivery via digital networks. Many educational publishers have already changed their sales models from selling individual books to selling site licenses for their materials delivered over networks.

Courseware will generally be more interactive, shifting control significantly towards learners. Design expertise for interactive materials does not currently reside either in the school system or with book publishers. Enormous opportunities are opening up for interactive authors and media designers to enter the education field. In their book *Interactivity by Design*, Ray Kristoff and Amy Satran write: "The one new variable... is the element of audience choice. And choice can take learners in unpredictable directions ... That's why interactivity calls for a greater commitment to planning, to usability, and to making the pieces work together."

New Courses

Courses will change dramatically in number, scope, and content. As education moves to student-initiated and just-in-time approaches, primary education will focus on teaching core competencies, which will include the ability to set up a personal study project, search databases, monitor your progress, and get assistance from tutors and teachers when necessary. Literacy, the ability to read and write text, will not be enough; students will also have to learn about still images, moving images, and graphic design, to reflect the change in media emphasis from print to visual materials.

Young students will learn to self-direct their learning, to work in teams, and to access learning materials and courses from networked digital libraries. At the River Oaks public school in Mississauga in 1996, I watched students in grades four, five, and six preparing their work for a United Nations Day school project. They were making posters to promote the event. Some drew pictures with pencils, crayons, and paints. Others used computer drawing programs to help get their ideas across. The students who used traditional materials scanned their artwork into computers so they could edit the images and add text titles and messages.

No student excelled at every aspect of the work. The computer whiz-kids helped their techno-deficient classmates with complicated software. The kids who could draw well helped their classmates who were not as artistically talented. The kids that were into design helped the others manipulate their images with bold borders, titles, and other graphic techniques.

At every step along the way, a teacher was available to help, but not necessarily by showing the kids how to use the equipment. Many of the students were much more knowledgeable about the technology than their teachers were. The teachers were the guides on the side, to make certain the students stayed on track, and to ensure that every student was allowed to contribute. The finished posters were printed out on color printers. The results were wonderful.

The students learned to work in teams, to let others contribute to their individual project, and to accept criticism. They also learned how to find the resources needed to complete their project, whether these were other students, images from the library, or help from their teacher. These bottom-up skills are exactly what businesses are looking for today from their employees.

That's what education is about. Computers and digital networks will not impart knowledge to students. They will, however, provide an excellent platform for a more comprehensive and student-centered learning process that will be coupled with mentoring by teachers and fellow students.

Teaching Teachers

The River Oaks example illustrates the need for teachers to modify their traditional roles in the classroom. No longer need the teacher be the source of accurate and comprehensive information in all subjects. It is no longer reasonable to expect that teachers will know all the answers; they never did anyway. Today teachers must concentrate more on process than on data. They need to be comfortable sharing some of their power with the students, acting as moderators and team leaders as frequently as they teach the lesson of the day from the curriculum.

It will be a huge task to train teachers how to function in their new roles. Young teachers will catch on quickly because they intuitively understand the paradigm shifts that are causing the Bagel Effect, but teachers who have been in the system for some time may have a difficult time adjusting. Retraining teachers will become a major task. Training materials for teachers will follow the same interactive designs as student materials and will help teachers get with the new paradigm as form, function, and information merge.

Students Teach Teachers

With change occurring so rapidly, it is common that some students will be more knowledgeable about a subject than a teacher. Many primary and secondary school students already know more than their teachers do when it comes to computers. Kids not only have more free time than teachers to bone up on subjects but they now have access to information about almost every subject imaginable. As they learn to search for and access that information, they will become more important resources in their own classrooms. The responsibilities of teachers as educational custodians will be relaxed as capable students are allowed to help both class-mates and teachers.

Students Teach Other Students

Peer-to-peer mentoring is one of the most natural learning experiences and will be recognized in a more formal manner. As students reach their teens and beyond, discussions among students and group assignments will become increasingly important. This will increase the depth of learning and also decrease the number of contact hours with instructors, a win-win situation for both students and school boards.

Digital networks will greatly facilitate student-to-student access using chat groups, newsgroups, e-mail, shared on-screen whiteboards, video-conferencing, and video-messaging. More advanced students will be available on-line at all hours to answer questions posed by less advanced students.

Self-Direction by Grade Ten

At a 1998 think-tank sponsored by the Minister of Education for Ontario, educators and business leaders suggested that curriculum-directed education would likely become less rele-vant after grade ten. By then, it was argued, students should have learned how to learn and be in a position to direct the balance of their own education with guidance from teachers and school resource persons.

This sounds as though secondary school students would be thrown to the wolves, but the facts tell a different story. Today's high school teachers and guidance counselors are not doing a satisfactory job of helping students plan their post-secondary lives. Too many students leave high school with-out motivation or a sense of purpose. Post-secondary institu-tions and businesses say students lack the basic knowledge and skills they need to thrive in their new environments.

Many school guidance counselors are out of touch with the reality of a career today. It is no longer associated with a job description but is the succession of jobs and unpaid activities that a person undertakes along his or her life path. Along with the current concept of a career comes a new set of abilities that one needs to be successful and these include the ability to motivate yourself, work well with others, deal with change, and learn new skills.

Learn What You Want

You'll learn what you want. New courseware will allow students to custom tailor their learning programs to their individual requirements. Instead of choosing a course based on set lectures, students will be able to more flexibly assemble their subject materials from lectures, documentaries, articles, and so on. In addition, they will be able to choose the depth with which they study a subject. Instead of spending three years completing algebra and trigonometry courses, a student will be able to study just those sections of algebra and trigonometry that may be necessary to, say, derive a formula for statistical analysis of focus group results.

Learn How You Want

You'll learn how you want. Standard courses at colleges and universities are currently provided in semester lengths with credit given for the number of class hours and lab/tutorial hours attended. These metrics are for the convenience of educational institutions, not students. They are not necessarily appropriate to the subject of study. If you buy a computer in mid November, that may be the moment of greatest motivation to enroll in a computer course.

As students take more responsibility for their learning they will increasingly pursue multiple paths to reach the same objectives. Some may enroll in a community college but take university courses to round out their learning needs. Others will do the converse. Still others will get credit for on-the-job learning that will count towards their diplomas and degrees. The question of core competencies will be a major issue of debate as institutions struggle to maintain graduation standards for students who will increasingly design their own mix of courses.

Learn Where You Want

You'll learn where you want. You might want to listen to a lecture on audiocassette while you're in your car, or watch a video at home, use a CD-ROM on your portable computer, or use a digital assistant on the bus. Students will match their context and available tools to a much wider range of media.

In-home learning will explode. As broadband networks connect a greater percentage of the population, some will take up flower arranging, others will study photography, and millions will learn to play musical instruments. Young couples will quickly log on to a parenting course after their child has a temper tantrum.

Accredited and certificated learning will increasingly occur in workplaces, malls, hotel rooms, and at home, as well as in classrooms. Digital networks, both wired and wireless, will be an equalizer for those living in remote communities, and the number of students that will have to live on campus in dormitories will decrease.

Many workers will train where they work. Large companies will formally enter the education business, offering courses to their employees for self-improvement. Union halls will become retraining sites where workers can pick up skills.

Learn When You Want

You'll learn when you want. Some students will continue to set aside their youthful years to get a basic education. Others will want to enter the work force earlier and pick up their formal education alongside practical experience. One in three postsecondary students already works while attending school.

For most, education will continue throughout life, at times appropriate for the learner. By 1995 less than half of Canada's university undergraduates were under the age of twenty-five. Adult students, most of whom who are part-time and non-residential, make up higher education's new majority. They will increasingly want to access courses at their convenience.

Giving control back to individuals will have a drastic impact on our lifestyles and life plans. Instead of being expected to graduate from high school and continue immediately with some form of post-secondary schooling, individuals will be able to follow their personal inclinations and receive education throughout their lives, whenever and wherever they choose.

Correspondence courses delivered through digital networks will flourish and become more affordable alternatives to universities, colleges, and private schools. All of these educators will compete for the same students, in contrast to the different demographics they serve today. Several Internet publishers currently offer education courses in a variety of subjects for as little as $5 a course, or an unlimited number of courses for a monthly fee of $20. Students will have a difficult time comparing the legitimacy and real value of different learning options.

Pace Yourself

Self-paced learning is one of the most important aspects of the educational change. We are all different, with our own intellectual strengths and weaknesses. One student may be a whiz at solving problems that require abstractions but not so good at practical work. With self-paced learning she might spend a disproportionate amount of time on her practical work, mastering it after many repetitions without the stigma of holding the class back with questions or receiving a low grade on a test score.

Self-paced learning tailored to individual students will become the norm. The development and production of interactive courses and reference materials will become a big growth industry. CD-ROMs and DVDs will be the initial delivery media, but schools will increasingly use digital networks to deliver centrally based courseware to any student at a terminal.

Corporate Courses

Large companies will set up their own courses certified by their own institutions. What organization is better qualified than Intel, say, to offer advanced courses in microchip design? Among the advantages of studying at Intel would be its access to internal experts who could be seconded for part-time teaching. In addition, Intel staff and students would get to know each other for potential follow-on employment opportunities.

Why shouldn't medical schools affiliate with hospitals instead of the reverse? Instead of studying at a medical school and doing your practical work at an associated hospital, hospitals will be certified in areas of expertise and students will travel to them to be certified in specialties ranging from microsurgery to physiotherapy.

Courses in automotive engineering might be best designed and conducted within an auto plant, ensuring that the skills developed will be matched to the industrial need. In this respect the new paradigm returns to the much older model of the craft guilds and apprenticeship system.

Course Modules

Instead of organizing education into years, semesters, and courses it will be organized into smaller units that better correspond to students' interests and needs. A single course module may correspond to a series of lectures or to a chapter in a book.

For example, if you are interested in French Impressionist paintings, you may wish to access courses on nineteenth and twentieth century European architecture, but only those modules that deal with France. By accumulating modules, students will be able to customize their own courses of study. These will increasingly be recognized for institutional credit provided they meet appropriate requirements. The modular learning approach will put a strain on institutions because, although they meet student needs, they are more difficult to administer than existing institution-oriented courses of study.

The new regime of user-centered courses of study will allow an entirely new type of course distributed among several institutions as students mix learning modules from different schools to assemble a single credit course. Instead of losing the political science student to Harvard because of its Kissinger lectures, Simon Fraser University will be able to keep the student by offering some learning modules in Vancouver mixed with some Kissinger lectures from Harvard. Post-secondary institutions will have to sort out who gets paid and how the fees are divided among themselves.

Focus on Facilities

Some educational institutions will survive by focusing on subjects that require expensive equipment. Since it's inconvenient to set up a chemistry lab or a metal-casting foundry, students will need to physically attend institutions to access these facilities. This will encourage institutions to offer courses that require physical resources as a way to keep enrollment up.

The original purpose of a university was a place for the most gifted and inquisitive, but this has given way to the right of every citizen to expect a university education. Universities will return to their former role as centers of excellence, for a smaller percentage of the population. Research will be a hallmark of public universities since it is not a profitable activity and requires public funding. Colleges and private sector institutions will assume the major responsibility for mass education.

BAGEL BITS

The biggest change in learning materials will be **course kits on demand.** Students and teachers will specify collections of articles, selections from texts, teachers' notes, videos, and so on. These will be assembled as books, CDs, and RAM cards at instant-print and bookstore venues. The content will be drawn from digital databases distributed among book and magazine publishers, television producers, and so on. Each specified content component will have an associated intellectual property fee that will flow to the owner of the copyright. Course kits put together in this way are already starting to appear at schools, although so far they have been restricted to text materials.

24 EARNING
Fewer Bosses, More Power

There has always been lots of work to do. Earning one's bread was originally just that, hunting and gathering food. As civilizations became more sophisticated, workers specialized into trades or became farmers, merchants, artists, innkeepers, soldiers, or the relatively few bosses who oversaw the work of others. Everyone except farmers had to barter for or buy their daily bread.

Work was done as needed. There was lots of planting in the spring and lots of harvesting in the fall, with much less work in between. Tailors worked longer hours when there was a wedding or ball coming up and fewer when there wasn't.

The Industrial Revolution brought with it jobs as we know them today. Owners, managers, and workers each had clearly defined jobs to do and they did them during regular working hours every day except Sunday. These jobs were more than just work. They brought with them frameworks for unions, frameworks for advancement, and frameworks for retirement.

Today a job has become a contractual matter, with legal recourse for discrimination in hiring, unfair dismissal, and job equity. As times are changing in reaction to the Bagel Effect so too is the definition of a job. Jobs today are defined in a much more flexible manner. Part-time employment is no longer a poor cousin to a full-time job. It is sometimes the preference of a worker who can use the balance of the work week for self-employment, education, or raising a family.

What Happened to Jobs?

Between 1980 and 1995, forty-three million jobs were lost to downsizing — a Bagel Effect. The generation Xers in the '80s and '90s were shaped by this period of recession and by the stock market meltdown. These events have changed the expectations of young people entering the work force. They no longer expect to earn more than their parents. They no longer expect an employer to look after their financial needs for a life-time, and they are more willing to take responsibility for their own welfare. In other words, they are more Bagel-savvy.

Television has been very good at mirroring social trends. In the '70s, the most popular sitcom was *All in the Family.* In that program, Archie Bunker was a blue-collar worker whose coarse pronouncements echoed the feelings of many workers. He called his son-in-law a lazy bum because he didn't have a job. In the '80s, the *Family Ties* series used the character of Alex Keaton, a young Republican, as the icon for America's move to the political right. The most popular sitcom in the '90s was *Seinfeld,* in which none of the four main characters held down a steady job for any length of time. By the '90s, casual employment from time to time was an accepted and appropriate lifestyle.

Focus on Workers

The new understanding of jobs is more centered on the work-er than the employer. Control and power are moving from the bureaucratic centers of organizations to the edges and that means there is more emphasis on the person performing the task and less on the manager.

This should not be confused with a shift in power from corporations to unions, since the Bagel framework views large unions, corporations, and governments as one side of the balance beam and workers, contractors, and taxpayers on the other. The new distinction is between bureaucratic organizations and individuals, with the former ceding power and control to the latter. In the new way of looking at things unions are not seen as necessarily representing individual workers and management is not seen as representing individual administrators. We're back to thinking about people, not their organizational proxies.

We Were Farmers

In 1906, the large majority of the Canadian work force — 86% — had jobs in agriculture. They provided our daily bread so efficiently that almost no one had to go hungry. By the middle of the twentieth century only 25% of Canadian workers had agricultural jobs. The other 75% worked in mining, forestry, manufacturing, and other industries.

By 1997, less than 3% of Canadian workers were still in agriculture. That small fraction, however, produced enough food to feed the entire population while creating a surplus, which was sold abroad. At the same time, less than 15% of Canadian jobs remained in the manufacturing and natural resources sectors. And these small percentages will decrease even further as technology continues to increase the productivity of workers in these areas.

The Service and Info Businesses

As agricultural and manufacturing jobs declined so dramatically, new jobs were created from the shift in economic value from tangible goods to information manipulation and services. In 1997, the large majority of workers — about 70% — were engaged in the service sectors. The fastest growing segment in this group has been information workers, who will comprise about half of the work force by the turn of the century.

My father worked in a factory making clothing with his hands and with machines. In the latter part of his life, he owned a small manufacturing company, but he still worked on the line, cutting garments from patterns and sending them off to operators who sewed them into finished goods. He never could grasp the concept of earning a living by any other means than producing something you could touch and feel.

Many of us have the same problem. The satisfaction that you get from growing something or making something is palpable. The satisfaction you get from putting a good deal together may be even more satisfying but understanding the benefit to society requires a much more sophisticated abstraction. One of the positive results of the Bagel Effect is that, as workers take more control of their jobs, they will better understand the value of what they do.

Organizations have flattened their administrative structures as a result of the Bagel Effect. That means there are fewer levels of administration and oversight, giving workers more freedom but also more responsibility. The accountability for work is passing to workers themselves. Many are functioning more like independent contractors who undertake to deliver services, solving problems that may crop up along the way.

The self-employed are seeing the results of flattened organizational structures as well. The television production business used to hire music composers to write music. Composers worked for music supervisors who were part of the production team. Nowadays composers are contracted to deliver a finished music score. They have to hire the musicians, book the recording studios, subcontract music copyists and arrangers, and so on. They get a larger lump-sum payment than they did in the '80s but they are responsible financially for any cost overages or other problems. Today they are no longer just composers but music contractors.

The move to contract out services relieves companies from many responsibilities associated with staff workers, including managing their human resources and providing sick and retirement benefits. We are witnessing a new mindset that focuses on talent-for-hire, reminiscent of the Middle Ages. In those days, tradespeople traveled from town to town, selling their crafts and services to a variety of clients. Today the talent-for-hire is just as likely to travel to the job virtually, on an electronic network, as to travel physically, but the concept is the same.

How to Succeed in Business

Whether you work for a company or work on your own, understanding Bagel-driven changes in the conduct and ethos of work will help you be more successful. Following are some principles for success that may be extracted from the Bagel Effect.

The workplace has less management and fewer supervisers than it used to have. Individuals have additional responsibility, within an organization, to organize their own work and to make certain they are productive when their assigned work is finished. The frequent reorganizations that accompany downsizing and restructuring mean that the job description you had yesterday may not fit what you do today. The work that was previously assigned to you may no longer be required of you or your department. If you wait to be reassigned work you may end up being classified as redundant and fired before that happens.

Find a way to be valuable to your company. Be a self-starter. Sitting around waiting to be told what to do is no longer an acceptable work ethic. Some of your colleagues will be overworked and overstressed. Help them out. Don't be concerned about whether the work you do is below or above your formal work rank.

Get Behind the Vision

Get behind your organization's vision. There will be more freedom for individual workers, but your energy should be focused on the organization's vision and objectives. Everyone should be pulling in the same direction, but you have the freedom to do so with more creativity and innovation than before.

The new corporate structure might look more like Duke Ellington's band in its heyday. Each instrument section (trumpets, trombones, saxes) needs a leader to set the interpretation, timing, and dynamics. Duke's band was filled with soloists, each of whom wanted to lead his section. They all wanted to play the lead part, not just a harmony part in the section (second-fiddle for you classical fans). One day, after Duke had a particularly trying rehearsal because of all the bitching about who would play the leads, he retitled all the music parts. Instead of *lead trumpet, trumpet 2, trumpet 3,* and *trumpet 4,* he retitled the parts *lead trumpet A, lead trumpet B, lead trumpet C,* and so on. Duke's little joke flattened his organizational chart and the humor lowered the tension for a few weeks.

CulTech Research Centre has a very flat organizational chart. There are no secretaries and no receptionists. The executive officer and I write and post our own letters. When we have a meeting, we all take turns bringing coffee. We do have management structures and reporting responsibilities but they are much reduced from what they might have been a decade ago.

When we pitch business, the people who will have to do the work are included in the final meetings. They are given the authority to deal directly with clients. This can only work if staff members are trustworthy to represent the organization and to look after the interests of both the client and the organization. This has been a difficult transition for some of us who came from environments that were much more polarized into management or worker job descriptions.

Change Is the Only Constant

Be flexible. The only environment we can expect to stay constant is the environment of change. Since change will be a constant during this period of structural upheaval, workers whose attitude is "that's not what I was hired to do" will be let go. The organization that hired you likely doesn't exist any more. If you can't find a comfortable place in the new organization, find other employment.

Learn to Learn

Within five years of accepting a job with an organization, you probably will be doing work you were not hired for. You must be able to learn new skills, or you will become less relevant. This is no different if you work for yourself. The concept of lifelong education applies immediately. The fishermen on the east and west coasts of Canada who are unwilling to learn a new trade when the fish run out are getting less sympathy from other Canadians who have seen the same thing happen to themselves or their friends in almost every industry.

While governments are refocusing their efforts on job retraining programs, it will be up to individuals to accept the inevitability of lifelong changes to their jobs. The idea that "you can't teach an old dog new tricks" will not wash in the new reality. Although the brain may not be at its peak in the second half of your life, the deficiency is more than made up for by your accumulated knowledge and experience. The most important thing you will ever learn is how to learn.

For Union Members

Large unions, like large companies, have had to adjust to increased input and far more control from their members. As a union member, you may be torn between a desire to contribute to the health of your company, and union regulations that keep you in a rigid job description and work jurisdiction. Big unions, like big companies and big government, must either adapt or die. Many unions are going with the flow and accommodating change from within. But if you're stuck in a situation where your union is at odds with your ability to contribute to your organization, bail out.

Contracting Out

From shipping clerks to high-level managers, workers are looking for opportunities to start their own business by contracting out services currently provided within an organization. Be on the lookout for situations where the structure of an organization prevents a task from being done as efficiently as you could do it on the outside. If you see such an opportunity, suggest to your boss that he investigate whether your company would be interested in such an arrangement.

We all have different personalities and emotional needs. The Bagel Effect suggests that these will be taken into account to a much greater extent in the future. Some of us want the security of guaranteed employment, regular work hours, automatic scheduling of vacations, and secure retirement plans. Others would trade those features for the freedom to control their place and hours of work, the ability to work for many employers, and the ability to control their savings according to their own investment strategies. For those others, becoming contractors is a happy alternative.

Working Extra Hours

Here's the reality. Non-unionized workers frequently work extra unpaid hours. Generally, the higher up the administrative ladder you go, the more additional hours you will work. The old paradigm of workers at the bottom being exploited for long hours of work so that the bosses can relax in cushy jobs has been turned upside down.

Most managers I've dealt with in industry give me their home phone numbers and are available at any time to answer questions. It is not unusual for executives to take their cellphones on vacation (I do) so they can be reached for comment and authorization, if a critical situation develops at work.

Even government employees, who for many years had reputations for working short shifts with long breaks, are spending more time with their noses to the grindstone. Again, the higher the position, the greater the additional effort. At the top levels of deputy minister and assistant deputy minister, the hours approach those of elected officials — work by day in the office and attend official dinners and functions by night.

Extra Hours for Entrepreneurs

Entrepreneurs who start their own businesses work even longer hours, with an accompanying blurring of the line between business and personal life. This may not be desirable, but it is a fact. If you are a person who wants a job with regular hours that does not intrude on your home life, you should aim for a lower- or middle-level position in a highly unionized company. Even if you take this route, don't count on job security, because the job or company may well vanish in a few years.

Ellie Ruben, vice president of the Bulldog Group, told me, "If you want to be successful you can't balance your personal and business life. Your work must come first."

New Jobs

The downsizing of large companies and governments in the nineties has skewed the availability of jobs significantly, and will continue to do so.

BAGEL BITS

Approximately five hundred managers were put out of work as a typical organization of ten thousand workers downsized to eight thousand workers in the '90s. These managerial jobs will not be created in other companies because all companies are flattening their administrative structures as part of the Bagel Effect's movement of power and control away from system centers.

Managers from large organizations are ill-suited to the needs of small businesses, which is the sector of the economy that is creating new jobs. Their skills have been honed to manage teams of ten to twenty people under their direct supervision and small businesses lack this structure entirely. As a result, tens of thousands of qualified workers, many of whom were in very responsible positions, are being put out of work with small prospects of finding other jobs for which they are trained.

The Growing Self-Employed

One job route for these ex-managers is to become self-employed, starting a consulting or contracting business where they can use the skills and knowledge acquired in their former jobs. Although they lack the job security and fringe benefits of their previous employment, they gain control of their working hours and can avoid stressful situations where they are trapped working with unsympathetic bosses or colleagues.

The benefits of controlling your own job destiny in a company you own or control can be more than worth the risks. The ability to balance your profits with the amount of personal and family activities you wish to pursue is very important to most self-employed people. And at the end of the day, your job is always secure so long as your company stays afloat.

Since many new jobs are coming from the manipulation of information, they are much more portable than those that depend on the location of land, resources, or factories. A growing number of people work from their homes, where they can increasingly connect to information resources as easily as in a downtown office or factory.

Working at Home

It is estimated that almost two million Canadians, almost a quarter of the working population, do some or all of their paid labor at home. Many are self-employed entrepreneurs who save money and travel time by working out of their homes. They are known as SOHOs — small office, home office. The balance work in large companies, part-time at a central office, part-time at homes. These are the telecommuters.

More than half the companies in North American now permit employees to telecommute. A third of those companies use their telecommuting programs as a tool to recruit employees, and three-quarters of the companies expect the use of telecommuting to increase.

AT&T did a cost/benefit analysis of six hundred telecommuters in 1996, which demonstrated an annual net savings of more than $11 million from reduced office rent and improved productivity — that's about $20,000 annually per worker.

Telecommuting creates isolation from your workgroup, and that has been its largest problem. As a result, the average teleworker lasts only about a year and a half working at home before opting to come back to the office. The next decade will see the implementation of videophones, video-messaging, and video-conferencing among home workers and at central offices. It is hoped that these social experiences, although mediated by technology, will alleviate the psychological problems associated with working from the home.

Work-at-Home Communities

While the growing trend of working at home is having a considerable impact on Canadian society, the planning and design of residential communities have not for the most part recognized it. The separation of home and work activities may be outdated for an increasing number of households, and residential planning which assumes that separation needs to be rethought.

In the Stonehaven wired community, the house exteriors are undifferentiated from others in the neighborhood, but the interiors have been designed with home working in mind. The changes in layout reflect the different traffic flows of home workers.

Each home has a separate entrance that allows workers and clients to enter and exit the house without interrupting or being interrupted by family traffic. It's possible to visit a home worker in Stonehaven and never meet the dog or kids. The home office has electrical connections prewired for a fax machine, a computer, telephones, and a modem. The developer offers turn key packages that can be completely configured and installed for work-at-home before you move in, saving considerable time and frustration for many workers taking advantage of this option.

In many cases workers, who have full-time jobs but feel they are at risk of losing them, are starting part-time businesses out of their homes for extra income while they keep their regular jobs. When such a home business reaches a critical income level, the worker quits the regular job, sometimes taking an early retirement package that serves as start-up capital for the home business venture.

Buying a Business

For many managers who are let go from their jobs with reasonable severance packages or early retirements, an existing business or franchise is just what they are looking for. They have the opportunity to use their managerial skills without the hassle of starting a new business, and the return on their investment is generally better than putting it in a secure bond or deposit certificate.

Pensions Pending

Folks who opt to start their own small business generally lack a business pension plan. This has become more of a worry since the government pension plans in Canada and the United States are being called into question by analysts who predict there will be insufficient funds available to pay the aging population "bulge" as it reaches retirement. A problem with government plans is that they are subject to the mood of voters and the state of the economy. Current proposals suggest that young workers may have to double or triple their contributions in order for retiring workers to get their pensions in coming years. Enacting and maintaining this sort of legislation is anything but assured.

BAGEL BITS

We will still have jobs in the future, but they are more likely to be defined over shorter periods of time, and we are more likely to change them frequently, with time off between engagements. As we move towards education and leisure pursuits that are spread throughout our lifetime, so will our work be spread out as lifelong earning.

The indications of lifelong earning are already evident: Co-op programs for high school and university students who work part-time in industries; mature workers coming back into the work force after retirement; young people frustrated by their lack of career direction; and almost all workers taking new training to prepare themselves for different assignments or new jobs.

As governments back away from supporting social programs, the arts, and sports activities, these areas will increasingly require volunteer workers. The volunteer sector already contributes unpaid work to the economy. People may not think of their contribution as work, but they work just as hard at volunteer activities as they do at their regular jobs.

In a future sitcom, Archie Bunker's successor is unlikely to scream at his son-in-law, "Get a Job!" He's much more likely to scream, "Get a Life!"

25 CONNECTED COMMUNITIES
Let's Get Wired

People Cause Change, Not Technology

It's fascinating to realize that the brain's computation capability is neither as fast nor as complex as computer systems, yet people are vastly superior to computers in terms of performing most useful tasks. To succeed in the coming century we need to understand the importance of how people act, react, and interact, not how bits are routed through networks.

Those who are concentrating on the new technologies themselves — the bits, the bandwidth, and the atoms of information transport — are missing the essence of the big change. Technology doesn't cause change, it only enables it. It's people who cause change.

Connected Communities

A key piece of new technology that will allow communities to be connected is the *gateway access box*. Different companies will brand it with different names but its functionality will be essentially the same in all its guises. The gateway accepts external signals that come to your apartment or home and converts them to a few standard types of signals, which are distributed to all the appliances within your home.

For example, cable TV, satellite TV, telephone service, modem service, and digital Internet can be connected to the gateway's inputs. The gateway converts these different signal types and protocols to just three standard signals for distribution in your apartment or home. The first is analog video, whose signals connect to your television sets, videorecorders, and videocameras. The second is digital Ethernet. This is the standard used to connect printers, computers, scanners, and all sorts of digital devices. The third is POTS — Plain Old Telephony Service. It connects to your phones and to your security system.

The three outputs of this gateway box connect to your Home Area Network — HAN — which in turn distributes these signals to devices scattered throughout your home.

Give Me a HAN, Please

The HAN is an idea whose time has come. A HAN consists of the various wires that carry the three types of signals and the gateway box. A HAN lets you distribute hi-fi and television signals to all the rooms of your home. Up until now you had to invest a great deal of money just to do this one function, and you still could not control your hi-fi or TV from your computer.

The same is true for the Ethernet computer network. Before its arrival, you could install a computer network but it would not let you control your home security system, home automation system, or hi-fi.

For the past two decades smart-home technology has been available to link your lighting, heating, and appliance systems together, but it has also required thousands of dollars of wiring behind the walls. Home security, one of the biggest growth industries, also requires wiring and transmitters throughout the home.

Because of the expense, few of these networks were ever installed in homes and apartments. If you did install one system (usually home security) you generally didn't go through the expense and bother of installing the others. In contrast, the new connected communities begin with wired homes in which *all* systems can talk to each other. What the HAN does in your home is deliver all of these signals corralled by the gateway box so that you can control them from PCs or TVs.

Home Automation

IBM recently brought to market a home gateway and HAN that recognize if someone is at the front door. The system is smart enough to check the house and sense if anyone is home. If not, the security camera at the front door takes a snapshot of the visitor and sends it over the Internet as an e-mail attachment to you at work. You receive an e-mail alert: "Someone is at your front door. Here's a snapshot. Would you care to send a message or would you like to speak with them directly?" Then through the Internet, either a signal is sent to play a recorded message, or a direct audio connection is made allowing you to speak to your visitor.

The same sensors that tell your home security there's an intruder, can now be linked to your home lighting system. You can set them to turn the lights on when you enter a room and turn them off shortly after you leave it.

Your home appliances can be connected to your computer system as well. When you leave your apartment and can't remember if you turned off the stove, you'll be able to phone your home and ask your system whether the stove is still on.

Integrated Phone, Video, and Web

Shortly after the start of the next century the telephone, Internet, and television networks will come together, making your life much simpler, allowing you to get rid of most of your remote controls, and integrating these services in a massive demonstration of Bagel Effect convergence.

The first step will be sending voice and fax over digital networks like the Internet. This is more than a cheap way to make phone calls. It will usher in a new range of services that were not available before. One of these will be a voice-enabled Web page.

BAGEL BITS

If a consumer is browsing a Web site and is interested in buying a product, she can click on an icon and connect directly to a customer agent who will carry on a telephone-type conversation and assist the customer with the sale. Add a video camera, and the relationship becomes more expressive.

Another application is *workgroup collaboration.* Students could use it for homework assignments or business could use it to conduct meetings at a distance. This application combines the power of phone calls, video-conferencing, electronic whiteboarding, and collaborative editing.

Unified messaging lets you listen to voicemail while surfing the Web, have your e-mail read over the phone to you while you're on the road, or have faxes automatically routed to your hotel.

A Connected Community

It may seem strange to suggest that technology will bring us closer to our family and friends but that is exactly what will happen as homes, schools, and places of work are increasingly connected.

In the Stonehaven connected community, people got to know their neighbors more quickly than in other places they lived previously. They used their videophones to interview potential babysitters and "looked in" on their kids while they were socializing at a neighbor's home. They e-mailed their neighbors to exchange information such as where to get a good auto mechanic and other typical over-the-back-fence neighborhood news.

One of the first messages on the community e-mail list was an invitation to all neighbors for a barbecue. The hosts provided food and the neighbors brought the drinks. Soon after they moved in, homeowners began sharing problems about their homes: the developer was late in finishing lawns and driveways, for example. The community residents formed an ad hoc consumers group to confront the developer en masse.

The developer, at first taken aback by the strength-in-numbers of the homeowners, soon found that it was more efficient to deal with common problems by explaining the situation on the community chat line than by making individual calls to each resident. The result was more power to the residents, but also a more informed developer who had better contact with his clients as a result of the new connectivity.

Personal Concierge

A few years back, Andersen Consulting did a survey asking which new services people would value most in a connected community. Topping the list were services that would be handled by a butler if you were rich, or by a concierge if you were at a hotel. They coined the term *personal concierge* to represent the automated assistant. People wanted help with time-consuming tasks, such as arranging ice time for a child's hockey team, ordering tickets for a play, finding a service to walk the dog when you go out of town, or arranging to have on-line shopping delivered. What many researchers are hearing is that consumers want value-added services more than just the bare-bones transactions themselves.

The New Consumer

The twentieth century brought with it the concept of industrialization and mass production. Henry Ford revolutionized auto-making by building many identical cars with just a few standard components. Although cars were inexpensive, they were available only in black. The new consumer is demanding more personalized products and services from suppliers.

The pendulum is swinging away from mass production and towards personalized production, a consequence of the Bagel Effect, which moves control to consumers and away from suppliers. Instead of choosing between a mass-produced off-the-rack suit and an expensive custom-made suit, imagine giving your measurements to a retailer and within a few days a factory delivers a suit that was altered to your individual measurements by robots and computers for a custom fit.

Consumer Health Services

Dramatic changes are occurring in all areas of private and public health service. The Bagel Effect is promoting a change in emphasis from disease treatment to health promotion, and the Internet is turning the public into self-motivated researchers.

Studies point to the improved ability of an informed consumer to manage his or her health and to make more effective use of health services. Preventable illness makes up about 70% of the cost burden to the health care system.

Medical studies have demonstrated that providing consumers with information and guidelines about taking care of their health can lower health care costs, frequently by 20%.

Personal Health Monitor

Each of us will have a private and confidential health information system that maintains a record of our height, weight, and all the tests we are given by doctors and clinics. We will be able to compare these with averages for the population at our age. Relevant videos and other materials will be provided to us in order that we may prevent health problems that we are prone to.

When you need to know if it's okay to take an aspirin while you are taking a prescription medication, you will access the same pharmaceutical references that your doctor and pharmacist have. You can see color photographs of pills and capsules that help to identify your prescription without having to wait for an appointment with your doctor or a visit to your pharmacist.

An enormous amount of health and wellness information already exists on the Internet. We do need authoritative network services that will validate trustworthy sources and weed out the quackery.

Documents

You can log onto the net today and access a standard will or incorporation document without going to a lawyer. Accessing government documents and information used to require phone calls, trips to government offices, and often user fees. Today you can download these through your browser instantly at no charge.

Many of the services that once required a lawyer or government agent today are being made available directly online, with corresponding savings in time and money. Non-contested divorces are one example. Driver license renewals are another. Little by little, we are taking back control over our home and work environments.

Financial Services

You can buy services today that let you do your checking and banking over the Internet, but they are awkward and not as secure as many would like. Soon, you will be doing all of your household finances and banking on a digital network that is secure, easy to use, and much less costly than banking is today.

Seniors

When you do retire, you will have more in common with young kids than with middle-aged workers. The old and the young share a greater amount of leisure than those in their working and family-building years.

In the past, people who retired had to think about taking up new hobbies or otherwise occupying their time. The new connectivity and access to masses of information means that you'll have the option to browse the world's accumulated knowledge until you find something that strikes your fancy, or you can continue in the same field in which you were active before, only at your own pace.

The curse of retirement is boredom and loneliness. Boredom is less likely when you are engaged in interactive pursuits that require you to think and act. Loneliness is less likely when you are connected to newsgroups and e-mail correspondents around the world.

A problem for some older people today is that new media are just that, *new*. Learning new technologies can be uncomfortable and frustrating. A great challenge for designers today is to bridge the technology gap, especially for the generation that did not grow up with digital tools. A recent University of Toronto class project led by Dr. Ron Baecker did just that. Multidisciplinary teams of students were charged with developing new applications to help older people. They had to work with focus groups of seniors, hone their ideas, and then build prototypes and test them with seniors. Some of the ideas were very innovative.

BAGEL BITS

One of the University of Toronto class teams invented a walking cane with a built-in global positioning sensor that uses satellite data to track your position on earth to within a few feet, like the automated maps in cars. The cane looked ordinary except for a large arrow in a bubble, like a compass needle. Seniors might use the cane to find their way home from a subway station, or to locate their car in a parking lot.

Seniors with failing memories will be able to subscribe to services that will send them an Internet e-mail alarm when it's time to take medication or pay a bill. Those who are physically impaired will be able to order staple groceries and meals delivered directly to their homes, and those who miss mahjong or poker games will be able to put together virtual on-line groups without having to brave the cold up north or the heat down south.

BAGEL BITS

Instead of building gated communities that protect residents by shutting out contact with the outside world, digitally connected communities promote interactions and participation among community members. This is a much healthier and happier approach, and will keep us more involved in life as we move on to our senior years.

26 LIFESTYLE
A Member of the Tribe

Technology will not change human nature. The basic tribal unit of ten to twenty individuals will continue to drive our greatest concerns. The primary such unit is the family. The next circle of concern and interest might be a religious group, a hobby group, a parent/teacher association, co-workers, or a local volunteer arts group.

Figure 26.1 — Circle of Friends

Connectivity to the world's information and people will not mean that we lose our sense of local identity. It will, in fact strengthen our need to belong to a few groups in which we feel comfortable with the people.

Families

Families will be shifting power and control down the administrative ladder just like organizations. The load of family responsibilities will be more evenly split among the family members and will be lightened by the availability of many online services that can be arranged from the home by different family members. The Bagel Effect will reverse the trend towards less personal contact among family members and allow for more time and more meaningful activities for the family.

BAGEL BITS

Many couples who participate in work-at-home programs several days a week are able to stagger their schedules so that one parent can be home each day to take the kids to school and such, eliminating the need for daycare and maintaining closer contact with their children.

Children will be more empowered to contribute to the family's needs. Much of this is happening with the use of the Internet, which is democratic with respect to age and gender. Kids are beginning to book travel tickets, search for a new family car, and even help to buy the new house.

The pressures of learning and earning and the fact that today both spouses often work have made it more difficult to arrange a convenient time to have children and enough time to bring them up. In general couples are having children later in life, more frequently in their thirties than their twenties and not unusually in their forties. The new lifestyle will co-mingle learning, earning, and family time. Spouses will take turns at each of these activities, better balancing the requirements of modern life.

Lifelong Leisure

Most of us understand leisure as something we *choose* to do as opposed to work, which is something we *have* to do. Because we're working more and learning more, we have less leisure time than before and it has become more valuable as a result. We are more conscious of waiting in lines, traveling to a store that doesn't have the item we need in stock, and waiting weeks for an appointment to trim the dog's hair.

We want to spend the time we *do* have free with our family and friends. Our leisure will be spread out differently throughout our lives. We may take a few years off work instead of a few weeks. Many people have more than one job. It is more important than ever to get away from the grind of the workplace in order to maintain a healthy emotional state.

As we all are different, some will want to spend the time in front of a large TV screen, some will want to go on family outings, and others will take university or training courses. Being surrounded by an increasing array of technology, many of us will opt for vacations that have no technology at all. Pristine beaches, rugged mountains, and wilderness areas will likely be at least as popular as they are now. Brochures will advertise areas that have no cellular phone service available.

In order to pay for this, we will likely work to an older age than we do now. Retirement will be triggered by a decline in health, not by age.

Music Lessons

The advent of broadband connectivity will make videophones and telepresence readily available. One outcome will be that home music lessons will become feasible even when the instructor is at a different location.

There are hundreds of music schools across the nation teaching the piano in classrooms with a single teacher and thirty or so students at electronic keyboards, listening to their playing and the teacher's comments on headphones. The teacher time-shares his attention and can tune in to each student's performance using a master switch. This type of activity can easily be extended over networks so students who don't live near a music school can have lessons.

Sports Simulations

The technologies developed for training airline pilots has been adapted by arcade games for simulating racing cars and the like. To date these have been targeted at youngsters, but the next decades will see simulation applications for all manner of sports so you can practice golfing, baseball, tennis, and skiing without waiting for a green, a diamond, a court, or a lift.

The use of simulators at sports centers and at home will further individualize the experience since you'll be able to tailor the course or game to your current level of experience and expertise. Again, the applications will be focused on you.

Gambling

If you fly first-class nowadays, you get a personal video screen that lets you choose movies and television on-demand, computer games, or an assortment of gambling simulations. These will be available soon in your home. The games are already on the net, complete with instructions and strategic suggestions. The addition will be betting real money and being able to transfer winnings directly to your Internet bank account.

This is a frightening thought for many, but it's in line with the increase in gambling parlors that are being authorized by governments across North America as a means of voluntary taxation. An important difference for Internet gambling is that there is no rake-off for governments because the servers can be located in tax havens. Presumably the odds will be better on-line as an inducement to gamblers.

Recently, my six-year-old grandson was staying with his parents in a hotel that offered Nintendo gaming on the television set. While he was flipping through the games he came across blackjack, the casino card game. He quickly learned the game, complete with betting strategies. His dad noticed what he was doing and had a chat with him about gambling but these activities could easily go unnoticed by parents. It won't be long before these games will move from a virtual betting account to your hotel credit card account.

Counseling

Think of your family and friends. Now think of some of the serious problems some of them have encountered in life. Substance abuse, broken marriages, depression, and so on. Each of us has sad stories that have touched our lives. One of the wonderful aspects of connectivity is access to support groups of every possible description.

A relative of mine has a young child that was kicked out of school for resisting the authority of his teacher. He's extremely bright, and is not a problem child at home. His mom went on the net and located a chat group of parents whose children had gone through the same problem at the same age. She made friends with some of the parents over the net and then met them socially. There was a wealth of information about his particular problem and how best to deal with it.

Although she had been to a professional counselor with her son, it was extremely helpful and comforting to find others that shared her interest and situation. The wonderful aspect about localization within globalization is that you have the largest sample from which to extract a small community of like interests. Even if your interest is narrow, chances are that you'll find a match.

Sex

Sex has been the most popular activity on digital networks since they were first deployed. There are sex newsgroups of every description. There are sex chat groups of every description. There are Web sites with sexy pictures of every description. And there are live video sites where people perform sex acts in front of cameras that broadcast throughout the net.

Some of the most popular CD-ROMs have been sex-related. You can play strip poker and watch a virtual partner disrobe. You can watch interactive movies in which the actions of the participants can be controlled by you — "take off your pants now."

You can have real-time chat sex, real-time phone sex, and real-time video sex virtually, with another person over the Internet.

You can't get AIDS and you can't get a venereal disease over a network or via a CD-ROM.

The government of Sweden passed a law that forbids making pornographic movies available in cyberspace that involve *simulated* children. Presumably they are concerned that someone will use computer graphics to construct a lifelike animated child and thereby bypass the restrictions on using real children for pornography.

Singles

Many maintain that it's safer to meet someone in cyberspace than in a singles bar. There has been a boom in using the Internet for social encounters. These include traditional singles services where you are paired with others of like interests or with characteristics you are looking for. They also include new virtual spaces where participants use avatars — graphical figures that represent the participants and whose attributes they can set.

One such virtual space, the Palace, allows users to construct a virtual house or mansion with rooms of any size and description. Participants then roam the premises, moving from room to room, making friends and acquaintances, and taking on roles they might be too shy to assume in real life.

BAGEL BITS

The Bagel Effect's bundle of component trends have resulted in a massive shift of control to individuals and a return to a freer society in which you can do much more of what you want with fewer regulations and restrictions.

According to the cyclic nature of this phenomenon, there are just a few decades remaining until we return to a more secure and regulated world. Enjoy it while you can.

AFTERWORD
Life Imitates Metaphor

"The Bagel is taking a bite out of the doughnut," read a July 10, 1998, article in the *Globe & Mail* ("Wax and Wane"). It went on, "In 1993, restaurants sold 561,000 bagels in an average two-week period. By 1997, that figure had jumped to 1.6 million. Meanwhile, doughnut sales took a dunking, falling from 3.4 million to 3 million in the same period."

The Bagel Effect emerged much like an artist's creation. It became self-evident once I removed the extraneous material surrounding it, much like a sculptor reveals the image inherent in a piece of wood or stone. Since it became manifest, the idea has struck sympathetic chords in a wide variety of people engaged in a wide variety of activities.

Early in 1998, the BBDO advertising agency contacted me and asked if I would submit a short essay for possible publication. One of their clients, Bell Canada, was running a series of corporate ads featuring independent discussions on the topic of communications and technology and wished to stimulate thoughtful discussion. I did a quick one-page précis of this book and sent it in. It was selected for publication and ran as a full-page feature in newspapers and magazines across the country. The agency extracted the title "The Bagel Effect" from the body of the essay.

I was then in the midst of a major disagreement with my publisher about the title of for this book. I was pushing for *The Bagel Effect* and they were resisteing it just as strongly. They believed *The Bagel Effect* title was confusing, misleading, and meaningless for potential customers. They also argued that the megatrend was a causal agent, not an effect.

My arguments were:

1. I liked the sound of *The Bagel Effect* title,
2. It's a simple metaphor that describes a complex process, and
3. Potential readers might be curious enough about what it means to browse the book.

I was losing the battle when the Bell Canada features hit the streets. The essay generated interest and readers remembered the title and got the gist of the meaning. A few days after the first ad ran, the publisher agreed to use *The Bagel Effect* title.

A Web site was set up so that netizens could read the essays in the series on-line and comment in a public discussion forum. The Bagel Effect essay generated the most comments by a wide margin. It was very exciting for me to get reaction directly from readers while I was still working on the book. Following are some samples of comments posted to the Web site forum:

> That profound shift is occurring in which more obsolete and inefficient members of our society lose — be it [the] less educated, the computer and Web illiterat[e], labor or big business... Wake up to [the] new era, seize new opportunities or be seized by those who do it better and faster... — *Yuri Gavris*

Over and over again, people voiced their concerns about the winners and losers in a world dominated by the Bagel Effect. The following comment voices this concern more strongly.

> Mr Hoffert, in his writing, has demonstrated the vast gulf that exists between our ruling elites, their philosophers and seers and we ordinary folk.
>
> ... Consider some on his list of losers. Big Government. If shrinking governments no longer have the powers to ensure public security, to restrain the arbitrary acts of the powerful, to provide for essential services, then the real losers are the ordinary Canadians.
>
> Big Unions. Unions have but one function — to enhance the welfare of their members ... Weaker unions means lower

> wages, less security and inferior — even dangerous — working conditions. Again, ordinary Canadians are the real losers...

> I do not see liberty and opportunity in the trends Hoffert trumpets. I see serfdom in these changes. I know that citizens are equal in a democracy but consumers are not all equal in a free market.... — *John McEwen*

Here was my first indication that some readers would see the Bagel Effect as an end I'm promoting, as opposed to a megatrend I'm noticing. Readers who are concerned about the negative impact of the Bagel Effect do not care that the predictions include a return to central authority and security in a quarter century. There is an important distinction made between democracy which posits equality for all citizens and free markets which this reader sees as biased against lower income groups. The Bagel Effect thesis does not view democracy and free markets as antithetical, but as complementary. This is congruent with the views of Canadian and American leaders, but clearly not in sync with all readers.

> The obvious concern is avoiding anarchy. Without a strong central authority, then who is responsible for establishing, maintaining and enforcing common values, standards, etc.
> — *Francis Cottier*

Anarchy is an emotion-laden word that seems to get everyone's attention. The Bagel Effect deals with trends and suggests that only a single system, the Internet, has managed to free itself from controls and only for a brief historical moment. We are in the midst of a relative trend towards anarchy, not in an anarchic state. The lesson I learned from reactions to the word is that, for maximum impact, I should have titled the book *Anarchy Among Us.*

> ... How do we get these visions of the future community out to the people at a faster rate than appears to be happening now? I [believe] that the golden resource of the next century is the human resource and yet I am concerned that we must communicate the vision to all demographics and all social levels...
> — *Dr. Karen Pappin*

The greater number of respondents were very positive about the opportunities available as a result of the Bagel Effect. They see the shifting power and control as empowering the current underclass and elevating it. This view is generally supported by the book's thesis, provided that access to interactive digital technology becomes ubiquitous, like television or telephones.

> ... What I would like to hear a lot more about is what is happening in the test market in Newmarket. ... What are the effects on peoples' behavior? What are they finding useful? Why? What are they doing differently or more of? — *d lang*

The most encouraging comments, and there have been many, make it clear that my message about the dominance of human nature over technological innovation has made it through the complex web of analysis and explanation.

The digital revolution, along with the convergence of many industries, media, and distribution networks, is an issue of burning concern for many. Important groups needed to help mold our new world feel threatened by the new technologies. Creators fear that computer programs will usurp their roles. Workers and managers fear they will lose their jobs because of convergence and downsizing. New technologies are seen as dehumanizing and removing people from social interaction. But the truth is that our ability to create and use technology is an essential differentiator between humans and other animals.

BAGEL BITS

The streams of downsizing, decentralization, deregulation, digitization, convergence, and interactivity that have inexorably joined to form the overflowing river of the Bagel Effect will just as surely lose their strength over the coming decades. What will remain, however, is the fundamental battle between freedom and security that is essentially human and essentially dynamic. Understand these forces and you will know the future.

INDEX

DATE DUE